Warrior • 21

Highland Clansman
1689–1746

Stuart Reid · Illustrated by Angus McBride

First published in Great Britain in 1997 by Osprey Publishing,
Midland House, West Way, Botley, Oxford OX2 0PH, UK
44-02 23rd St, Suite 219, Long Island City, NY 11101, USA
E-mail: info@ospreypublishing.com

Transferred to digital print on demand 2009

First published 1997
10th impression 2008

Printed and bound by Cadmus Communications, USA

A CIP catalogue record for this book is available from the British Library

ISBN: 978 1 85532 660 6

Military Editor: Iain MacGregor
Design by The Black Spot
Filmset in Great Britain

Dedication and Thanks
To the Wallace Clan Trust.

Author's Note
A number of the illustrations in this study are copied from a quite remarkable series of sketches drawn by an unindentified artist in the
Penicuik area at the time of the Jacobite occupation of Edinburgh in 1745. Readers wishing to see the originals – and many others
besides – can find them reprodcued in *Witness to Rebellion: John Maclean's Journal of the Forty-five and the Penicuik Drawings*,
edited by Ian Browne and Hugh Cheape. (See Bibliography)

Artist's Note
Readers may care to note that the original paintings from which the colour plates in this book were prepared are available for private
sale. All reproduction copyright whatsoever is retained by the Publishers. Enquiries should be addressed to:
Scorpio Gallery, P.O. Box 475, Hailsham, E.Sussex, BN27 2SL
The Publishers regret that they can enter into no correspondence in this matter.

Front Cover
A section from David Morier's *An Incident in the Rebellion of 1745*
(The Royal Collection © 2001 Her Majesty Queen Elizabeth II)

FOR A CATALOGUE OF ALL BOOKS PUBLISHED BY OSPREY
MILITARY AND AVIATION PLEASE CONTACT:

Osprey Direct, c/o Random House Distribution Center,
400 Hahn Road, Westminster, MD 21157
Email: uscustomerservice@ospreypublishing.com

Osprey Direct, The Book Service Ltd, Distribution Centre,
Colchester Road, Frating Green, Colchester, Essex, CO7 7DW
E-mail: customerservice@ospreypublishing.com

www.ospreypublishing.com

HIGHLAND CLANSMAN 1689-1746

INTRODUCTION

Duncan Forbes of Culloden provided one of the clearest definitions of a Highland Clan in 1746, describing them as "a set of men all bearing the same surname and believing themselves to be related one to the other and to be descended from the same common stock. In each Clan, there are several subaltern tribes, who owe their dependence on their own immediate chief, but all agree in owing allegiance to the Supreme Chief of the Clan or Kindred and look upon it to be their duty to support him in all adventures." Hardly pausing to draw breath, he went on to grumble: "As those Clans or Kindreds live by themselves, and possess different Straths, Glens or districts, without any considerable mixture of Strangers, it has been for a great many years impracticable (and hardly thought safe to try it) to give the Law its course amongst the Mountains."

Forbes, as lord president, had a very proper concern for the maintenance of law and order, but the Highland Clans were not just a threat to the civil peace. Between 1603 and 1746 they played an increasingly prominent role on battlefields both at home and abroad.

CHRONOLOGY

NB: All regiments and companies below are regularly recruited units as distinct from Clan levies. A considerable number of other units more or less substantially raised in the Highlands during the Civil War period are also omitted. The dates refer only to the first authorisation to recruit the named units. In some cases, particularly for the 'Dutch' regiments and the Royal Scots, recruiting parties were active in the Highlands and the rest of Scotland throughout the period under discussion.

Those events marked with an asterisk saw Highland Clansmen engaged on both sides.

1574	Scots/Highland Regiment recruited for Dutch service
1603	King James VI of Scotland becomes James I of Great Britain; Buccleugh's Regiment raised for Dutch service
1624	Two Highland companies raised for policing duties
1626	Mackay's Regiment raised for Danish service (later Swedish)
1631	Hamilton's Regiment raised for Swedish service
1633	Hepburn's Regiment (later Royal Scots) raised
1639	1st 'Bishop's War'*
1640	2nd 'Bishop's War'*
1644	29 Aug Royal standard raised by Montrose at Blair

David, Lord Ogilvy (1725-1803). Eldest son of the Earl of Airlie, he raised a Jacobite regiment after Prestonpans, marched with it to Derby and escaped to Norway after Culloden. Given permission to raise a regiment for the French Army, he employed a number of the officers who had served under him in 1745/6. The regiment was disbanded in 1763 but Ogilvy rose to become a lieutenant-general in the French Army before receiving a pardon and returning home as Earl of Airlie in 1778. The red and black tartan worn in this portrait appears to have been very popular (with the gentry at least) in the 1740s, and variations appear in a number of other contemporary portraits. [Private Scottish collection]

	1 Sept Battle of TIPPERMUIR
	13 Sept Battle of ABERDEEN
1645	*2 Feb* Battle of INVERLOCHY*
	9 May Battle of AULDEARN*
	2 July Battle of ALFORD
	15 Aug Battle of KILSYTH*
	13 Sept Battle of PHILIPHAUGH
1646	*14 May* Battle of ABERDEEN
1647	*24 May* Alasdair MacCholla defeated at RHUNAHOARINE
1650	*27 April* Battle of CARBISDALE*
1667	*3 Aug* Highland company raised for policing duties
1675	Wauchope's Regiment raised for Dutch service
1677	*6 Sept* Second Highland company raised
1681	*15 April* Both Highland companies incorporated in Earl of Mar's Regiment (Scots Fusiliers **1685** *20 Nov* Highland company added to Scots Guards
1688	*4 Aug* Highland companies defeated at MULROY*
1689	*18 April* Argyll's (Highland)Regiment raised; Grant's (Highland)Regiment raised
	25 April Laird of Greenock's Highland Company raised
	18 May Jacobite Clans muster under Dundee at Dalcomera
	27 July Battle of KILLIECRANKIE*
	21 Aug Battle of DUNKELD
	23 Aug Existing Menzies Highland Company taken on regular establishment
1690	*1 May* Battle of CROMDALE*
	16 July Menzies Company incorporated in Hill's Regiment
1691	*February* Two Highland companies raised: Munro and Wishart
	May Two Highland companies raised: Lumsdaine and Mackay
	August Captain Archibald Murray's Highland Company raised
1694	*April* All Highland companies drafted into Moncrieff's Regiment
1701	*24 June* Two Highland companies raised under Campbell of Fonab and Grant of Ballindalloch
1704	*1 June* Duncan MacKenzie's Highland Company raised
1715	*6 Sept* Jacobite standard raised at Braemar
	13 Nov Battle of SHERIFFMUIR
1717	Highland companies disbanded
1719	*9 June* Battle of GLENSHIEL*
1725	*12 May* Six Highland independent companies authorised
1739	*25 Oct* Independent companies embodied as 43rd Highlanders
1744	*1 Aug* Royal Ecossois raised
1745	*8 June* 64th (Loudon's) Highlanders raised
	19 Aug Jacobite standard raised at Glenfinnan
	21 Sept Battle of PRESTONPANS*
	1 Oct Highland independent companies and Argyll Militia authorised
	23 Dec Highland independent companies defeated at INVERURIE*
1746	*17 Jan* Battle of FALKIRK*
	16 April Battle of CULLODEN*

Rear view of a Highland Clansman 1745, after one of a remarkable series of contemporary illustrations of Jacobite and Loyalist troops sketched by an unknown artist in the Penicuik area. Note that he is armed only with a firelock and bayonet rather than the broadsword and targe traditionally associated with Highland troops. [Author's collection]

The Highland Clans

While it would certainly be true to describe the Scottish Highlanders as a warrior people, it would also be quite wrong to casually assume that every man in that society was a warrior. On the contrary, like most, if not all, warrior societies, the Clans were actually comprised of an agricultural peasantry dominated by a warrior aristocracy.

At the head of the Clan stood its 'chief', whose single most important function was to lead the Clan in time of war. Obviously this was not always possible: according to circumstances his place might be taken by a younger brother, or even a son, if he was too old or infirm to lead the Clan levy in person; if he was too young, his place would normally be taken by his guardian or 'tutor'.

Next in order of importance came not his immediate family – brothers, cousins and the like – but the heads of the various branches of the Clan, usually, but not always, founded by younger sons of previous chiefs. Naturally such a profusion of men each bearing the same surname could at first sight lead to confusion, but there was a simple remedy. To take the example of the Grants: The Clan chief was quite properly known simply as Grant, the Chief of Grant, or the Laird of Grant. His 'vassals' (for want of a better term) were also named Grant, but to identify one from another they were addressed not by their surname, but by the name of their estate or farm. In formal documents this might be set down as, say, John Grant of Sheuglie, but in everyday usage the designations alone sufficed – Sheuglie, Milton, Corriemony, Ballindalloch and so on. This practice can still occasionally be found today in rural Scotland. While this might at first sound confusing, it is in fact a great deal less confusing than trying to distinguish between several dozen contemporary or near contemporary John Campbells, Kenneth MacKenzies and Patrick Grants; far less the innumerable Donald MacDonalds.

Sons were similarly described. In 1745 the Argyle Militia was raised by General John Campbell of Mamore but actually led in the field by his son Colonel John Campbell, younger of Mamore. Some confusion might arise as to whether the father or the son was being referred to, but in this particular case it seems to have been avoided by simply referring to the younger Mamore as 'Colonel Jack', although he was obviously a prominent enough figure to get away with it. The only real confusion which can arise is where it became necessary to appoint a tutor, or guardian, to a young chief or head of a family. Although he might otherwise be known by his own name and estate, this gentleman was also referred to by his office for so long as he held it. Thus Sir James Fraser of Brea, who died in 1650, in his private capacity was known simply as Brea, but as the temporary leader of his Clan he is also simultaneously known to history as The Tutor of Lovat.

Generally speaking, all or most of these vassals held their lands by means of a charter granted by their chief, or occasionally by his feudal superior. In practice most Clan chiefs either studiously ignored the imposition by the Crown of feudal superiors, or even actively opposed

James Francis Edward Stuart (1688-1766). The son of King James VII of Scotland, his birth in 1688 precipitated the so-called 'Glorious Revolution'. All the subsequent Jacobite risings were, ostensibly at least, aimed at placing him upon a combined throne for Scotland and England. [Author's collection]

Dr. Archibald Cameron (1707-1753), younger brother of Donald Cameron of Locheil and lieutenant-colonel of his regiment 1745/6. Although he escaped to France after Culloden, he was arrested and executed in 1753 while attempting to recover some of the Loch Arkaig gold. Note that although he occupied an important place in his Clan's hierarchy, he has not chosen to be depicted in Highland dress. [Scottish National Portrait Gallery]

them. Whatever their title, the chiefs in turn let much of it out on leases or tacks to the next social strata – the *tacksmen*, also distinguished mainly by the name of their farm. Sometimes these tacks might be carried over for generations until the families concerned, although retaining their own surnames, became accepted as septs of a particular Clan. Thus the MacRaes tended to follow the MacKenzie Earls of Seaforth, the MacColls were generally accounted among the Appin Stewarts and the MacBeans were bound to the Lairds of Mackintosh. Apart from these and other similar examples, it is unlikely that such relationships were as formal as today's tartan salesmen like to pretend. Indeed, it was far from uncommon for a *tacksman* to bear the name of another 'established' Clan entirely. MacDonell of Glengarry's Regiment in 1745 included Grant, Mackay and MacKenzie officers and the former at least, from Glen Urquhart, were long-standing followers of Glengarry, frequently at odds with their own chief on the other side of Loch Ness.

It was even quite possible, to quote an extreme example, for a MacDonald to hold a tack from a Campbell. In 1636 the infamous Coll

Ciotach accepted a tack of Colonsay from Archibald Campbell, Lord Lorne. In addition to a cash rental, Coll Ciotach bound himself to serve Lorne faithfully in all his lawful employments and affairs in the Highlands and Islands, by both land and sea. In this particular case the tack, accepted under considerable duress, led to trouble, but it was absolutely typical in imposing upon the *tacksman* an obligation for military service.

Armed clashes between one Clan and another tended to involve little bloodshed: and might be confined to a series of raids and counter-raids aimed at running off the flocks and herds of the opposing party. If the raiders were intercepted either on the way in or the way out, a violent clash might occur, but otherwise pitched battles were something of a rarity.

While cattle raids have always been the stuff of Gaelic legend, "committed by those who did not regard them as dishonourable, but exercised them at all times, as the means of weakening or punishing their enemies", they were principally carried out by a class of men known as *cearnachs* – or *caterans* in Lowland Scots. The term simply means 'soldier', and in origin is similar to the Irish *kern* (although in character they were actually closer akin to the Irish *buannacht*). Drawn from no particular strata in Highland society, they were by all accounts wild enough, and were employed for killing, burning and even occasionally for fighting! As in Ireland, they had something of a reputation as swaggering bullies, and their bands often enough included 'broken men' owing allegiance to no particular Clan.

"In their best days," wrote Stewart of Garth, "the cearnachs were a select band, and were employed in all enterprises where uncommon danger was to be encountered, and more than common honour to be acquired. Latterly, however, their employments were less laudable, and consisted in levying contributions on their Lowland neighbours, or in making them pay tribute, or *Black Mail*, for protection. The sons of the tacksmen, or second order of gentry, frequently joined these parties, and considered their exploits as good training in the manly exercises proper for a soldier."

The *cearnach*, rather than the Clan gentry, probably conformed most closely to the popular stereotype of the Highland Clansman, and supplied most of the mercenary soldiers who served all over Europe before the British Army claimed them for its own. If the Irish comparison can be taken further, it would seem reasonable to suppose that while the Clan gentry were armed with broadsword and targe, the *cearnach* were armed with Lochaber axes and the like.

These men did not, however, represent the lowest strata in Clan society. There were also *ghillies*. Again like their Irish equivalents, these were outdoor servants rather than soldiers, although they could fight when the occasion demanded. The ordinary Clansman was not really

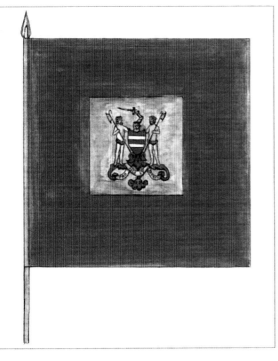

This banner is said to have been carried by Locheil's Regiment during the '45, although it may actually have belonged to Cameron of Glendessary. While the Cameron arms are depicted on the green central panel, the crest is an arm and sword, not Locheil's sheaf of arrows. The rest of the banner is red and this would seem to accord with a 1689 reference by James Philip of Almerieclose to "Glendessary's ruddy banner". Locheil's own banner may well have been captured at Culloden, for one comprising red and yellow horizontal bars was in private hands in the last century. [Author's collection]

a warrior at all and was levied out only in an emergency, and even then for as short a time as possible. Those men levied out during the '45 and imprisoned in its aftermath seem to have been a very sorry collection indeed, made up of old men and young boys, herdsmen, boatmen, labourers and ploughboys who for the most part were virtually unarmed.

Contemporary etching of Jacobite troops parading outside Holyrood House in 1745. The troopers on the left wear hats and presumably represent the Prince's Lifeguard, in blue coats turned up with red. Note how the Highlanders on the right are all armed with firelocks and bayonets.
[National Museums of Scotland]

ORGANISATION

At the most basic level, organisation could be little more than a matter of half a dozen *cearnach* or *ghillies* packing in behind a *tacksman*. A *creach*, or cattle raid, might involve two or three *tacksmen*, backed up with a gang of *cearnach* and accompanied by a few *ghillies*, whose principal function was not to fight, but to drive any livestock which might be lifted.

When there was a more general levying out, which called for the full strength of the Clan to be deployed onto the heather, a fairly conventional military structure was adopted and the Clansmen were mustered into companies and battalions. At least three of the Jacobite regiments raised in 1745 – Glengarry's, Locheil's and Ogilvy's – even had grenadier companies, although no record appears to have survived as to how they might have been distinguished from other companies in their battalions.

In theory the Clan gentry provided the officers, while the *cearnach*, naturally enough, became sergeants or filled out the front ranks; in practice it was rarely so neatly or thoroughly organised, as Colonel Sullivan, the Jacobite adjutant general, recalled:

"All was confused," he wrote, describing the levies who assembled at Glenfinnan in August 1745. "They must go by tribes; such a chiefe of a tribe had sixty men, another thirty, another twenty, more or lesse; they would not mix nor seperat, & would have double officers, yt is two Captns & two Lts, to each Compagny, strong or weak. That was uselesse, & became a great charge afterwards to H.R.Hs. They wou'd follow their own way, but littel & littel, were brought into a certain regulation."

That "certain regulation" included the amalgamation of non-viable units or, in extreme cases, their incorporation within larger units. The small MacLean contingent, for example, went through most of the '45 attached to the Atholl Brigade but at Culloden formed a composite battalion with the MacLachlans. However, in common with other rebel armies throughout history, such pragmatic measures did not extend to redundant or under-employed officers relinquishing their commissions. Glengarry's Regiment shared two lieutenant-colonels, four majors, 14 captains and at least 15 other officers – and even this is clearly something of an underestimate since a good half of them only represent the Glen Urquhart officers.

CLOTHING

Unlike more conventional forces, Highland armies were rarely in a position to issue clothing either to the officers or to the rank and file, but it did happen occasionally. At Christmas 1745 the citizens of Glasgow were ordered to supply the Jacobites with "6000 cloth short coats, 12000 linnen shirts, 6000 pair of shoes, 6000 bonnets, and as many tartan hose". After their march to Derby and back they were no doubt sorely in need of these items. Further north, Lord Lewis Gordon and his officers were scouring the countryside for plaids as well, but they were attempting to provide Highland clothing for men who normally wore breeches, since a conscious decision had been taken by the rebel leaders to clothe all their men as Highlanders, irrespective of their actual origin.

Highland dress could take a number of forms, although it is important to appreciate that before they were encouraged to it in the late 18th century, few if any Clansmen and fewer still of the gentlemen had any objection to wearing breeches if they were available. Indeed, breeches were as common as the kilt in Sutherland and in the Hebrides. While comic-book and film stereotypes frequently portray Clansmen striding forth clad in little more than a ragged shirt and a plaid, such clothing is hardly adequate for the harsh weather conditions the Clansmen encountered in the hills.

An interesting picture of how the ordinary Highlander actually dressed is provided by the body of an unknown youth, murdered and buried in a peat bog on Arnish Moor on the island of Lewis. It dates from around the beginning of the 18th century. The patched and ragged condition

These illustrations, based on the Penicuik sketches, are the only known representations of the Jacobite Hussars raised by John Murray of Broughton in 1745. Contemporary descriptions refer to their wearing "plaid" waistcoats and reddish fur caps. Both troopers depicted here also wear shoulder plaids.
[Author's collection]

of his clothing precludes any thought that the murder victim was well off. Aside from the fact that he was not wearing breeches (this may suggest that he had a plaid, although Edward Burt[1] describes and illustrates Clansmen simply wandering around in their shirt tails) he would by any normal standards be considered adequately dressed. On the body were found two woollen shirts, worn one on top of the other, and a hip-length woollen coat lined with the remains of an older one. There was also a

---

1 Edward Burt has never been positively identified but travelled widely in the Highlands in the 1730's and is believed to have been employed in General Wade's road building programme.

James Drummond, Duke of Perth (1713-1746). Appointed a lieutenant-general in the Jacobite Army in 1745, Perth was personally popular, but no match for the haughty and ambitious Lord George Murray. In poor health during the campaign, he died on board the ship that was carrying him to exile in France. [Grimsthorpe and Drummond Castle Trust]

Les Montagnards d'Ecosse en
leur habits accûtumés avec
un manteau pendant.

Berg-Schotten in gewohnlichen
Aufzug mit herab hangen:
der Decke.

Un Montagnard d'Ecosse qui prend son
manteau sur les epaules quád il va pleuvoir.
Ein seine Decke gegé dé Regé gleich
eine Mantel über die Schul:
tern schlagender Berg
Schott:

Johañ Christian Leopold excudit Auguste Vindelicorr

Three useful rear views of the plaid and short Highland coat, by Johan Christian Leopold. [National Museums of Scotland]

knitted blue bonnet on his head and a rather long pair of stockings on his legs. A slightly older corpse recovered from a peat bog at Quintfall Hill in Sutherland was wearing a plaid rolled over his shoulder, two pairs of breeches and two jackets, and may have had a linen shirt underneath.

There were essentially four garments peculiar to Highland dress. The first and most famous was the belted plaid, traditionally comprising six double ells of tartan material. At this point it should be pointed out that a Scots ell measured only 37in (95cm) and that a double ell was twice the usual width, not twice the length. Ordinarily plaiding was woven on a 27in (68.5cm) width and two pieces had to be sewn together to achieve the normal broadcloth width of 54in (137cm). Even so, six yards of material is quite a length, but Stewart of Garth quite explicitly states that it was folded in half to double the thickness before it was put on.

The plaid was normally pleated and belted around the waist so that the bottom hem rested just above the knee. The surplus material was draped over the shoulders. Pleating a plaid can be a tedious business, and although it is best done on a table or other flat surface raised above the ground, if a neat and tidy appearance is not required, the plaid can just as easily be thrown over the shoulders and then gathered in at the waist. The end result is far from elegant, but it does work and bears a very convincing resemblance to many contemporary illustrations. In whatever manner it was put on, historians of Highland dress are curiously prone to dating its introduction to the latter part of the 16th century, but there seems absolutely no reason to doubt that numerous earlier references to "mantles" also relate to belled plaids.

A late development of the plaid was the *philabeg*, or kilt. This was made simply by taking a single width of plaiding and sewing the tops of the pleats in place. To judge by surviving 18th century examples it was a

Not all Highlanders wore the kilt. The clothing worn in this reconstruction is made up to a pattern taken off clothing found on a 17th century body discovered in a peat-bog at Quintfall Hill in Caithness. The man was wearing two suits, one on top of the other, and had a shoulder plaid too.
[Author's collection]

very different garment from the modern kilt and was made up from a full width (27in) of plaiding. The upper hem reached as far as the bottom of the rib-cage, and the pleats themselves were little more than gathers, bearing no resemblance to the familiar deep knife-edged pleats introduced in the early 19th century. The precise origin of the kilt has been a source of some controversy. In so far as it was discussed at all during the 18th century, it was generally accepted to have been devised by an Englishman named Rawlinson who worked in Lochaber in the 1720s. Many subsequent (non-contemporary) writers have disputed this, although no reliable evidence of the kilt's use prior to the early 18th century has surfaced, and it is hard to escape the impression that there would not be an argument at all had the supposed inventor not been an Englishman!

In the British Army the kilt was introduced to Highland regiments as a fatigue garment in about the 1750s, and it only gradually replaced the plaid in the latter half of the 18th century. Prior to its widespread adoption, Highlanders who found the plaid impractical either wandered around in their shirt tails, turned instead to breeches – especially for boat work – or wore tartan trews.

The trews, or *truibhs*, were essentially a form of hose. Although similar non-patterned garments were worn in Ireland, in Scotland they were always made from tartan material. Usually, but not invariably, the material was cut on the cross to give the necessary flexibility at the knee, incidentally producing a diagonally placed check. Originally, like mediaeval hose, they comprised fairly close-fitting leggings with integral feet. Unlike hose, however, they generally had garters tied below the knee, partly for support – since the waistband was not laced into a pourpoint and tended to "hing aff the arse" – and partly to prevent unsightly "bagging" around the knees. Martin Martin from Skye described them thus in 1703:

"Many of the People wear *Trowis*, some of them very fine Woven like Stockings of those made like of Cloath; some are coloured, and others are striped; the latter as well shaped as the former, lying close to the Body from the middle downwards, and tied around with a Belt above the Haunches. There is a square piece of Cloth which hangs down before."

A few 18th century illustrations of trews show them separated into knee breeches and more-or-less matching stockings. This may simply

Officer and sergeant of an early
Highland regiment by Van Gucht.
[Author's collection]

13

2nd Battalion colour, Lord Ogilvy's Regiment 1745/6 – saved from capture at Culloden. Blue with white saltire and scroll. Thistle in natural tinctures. [Author's collection]

reflect a more modern style, or perhaps it was intended to facilitate the wearing of riding boots, which in turn had become necessary when large 'riding horses' were introduced in place of the traditional 'Thelwell-like' shelties or Garrons. For obvious reasons trews were the preferred form of dress for riding, although it was not unknown for hardier souls to ride wearing a plaid – one of the contemporary Penicuik sketches depicts old John Gordon of Glenbucket doing just that.

The wearing of trews was not by any means confined to horsemen: some illustrations show them worn in conjunction with the plaid in bad weather. They did indicate status too: while the ordinary Clansman had his plaid, a gentleman could afford to have a tailored pair of trews.

Since the plaid doubled as a cloak (and bedding), there was no great incentive for the Highlander to wear a long coat, although a knee-length or longer sleeveless tartan coat is worn by about half the Clansmen in the mid 17th century Stettin prints and appears to be associated with the northern Highlands. Instead, short waist- or hip-length jackets were worn. (Longer ones would have been difficult to wear with a belted plaid.) In the 17th century a single coloured jacket seems to have been the norm, and green or blue ones are reported to have been particularly popular, but in the 18th century tartan jackets predominated.

As for the tartans themselves, it may be as well to begin by asserting that there is no evidence for the use of Clan tartans in the modern sense. Indeed, it is a touch disconcerting to find that while most current Campbell setts are based on the dark blue Black Watch sett, most 18th century Campbell sitters sport bright red tartans. There is perhaps more evidence for the existence of 'district' setts – patterns traditional to certain areas and heavily influenced by the local availability of natural dyestuffs.

George Buchannan, writing in 1581, says: "They delight in variegated garments, especially stripes, and their favourite colours are purple and blue. Their ancestors wore plaids of many colours, and numbers still retain this custom, but the majority now in their dress prefer a dark brown, imitating nearly the leaves of the heather, that when lying upon the heath in the day, they may not be discovered by the appearance of their clothes."

While camouflage was no doubt a consideration, the brighter dyes would also have been more expensive and so would have been available for the most part only to the Clan gentry. Nevertheless, there is some interesting evidence to suggest that an embryonic form of Clan tartan may have emerged towards the end of the 17th century. In his description of the great gathering of Jacobite Clans at Dalcomera in 1689, James Philip of Almerieclose makes various references to the followers of this chief or that wearing plaids with a red stripe, or a triple red stripe, or a yellow stripe and so on. This suggests that while, like everyone else, they were wearing brown, green or bluish plaids, according to their own 'fancies', those *cearnach* in the service of a particular chief may have indicated their allegiance by weaving in a thin brightly coloured over-stripe, using yarn supplied by that chief.

Equipment

By and large the Highland Clansman was little encumbered by equipment. He tended to wear all of his clothing – and, of course, his bedroll – and contemporary observers frequently commented upon the fact that if they did carry anything too large to fit in the purse, or sporran, they simply bundled it up in the folds of their plaids.

Nevertheless, there were certain basic requirements which had to be met. Chief among them was some means of carrying food. Happily this was a relatively straightforward matter in that the Clansman's staple diet was oatmeal, cooked in a variety of ways or *in extremis* eaten raw. An English Parliamentarian tract in 1644 declared: "The Scots desire nothing but meale, of which they boast they can make nine severall dishes."

To carry this meal, all that was required was a simple linen bag (probably hidden in the plaid), although in 1745 Lord George Murray arranged for the manufacture of proper haversacks for his men. Tin canteens were also provided at the same time, but this seems to have been quite exceptional. Some basic cooking utensils must have been carried in order to produce some of those "nine severall dishes" and at the very least these would have included thin iron plates or girdles on which to cook oatcakes, and perhaps small cast-iron porridge pots.

Highlanders appear to have worn little armour; ordinary Clansmen probably wore none at all. There is abundant evidence for the early use of simple helmets and mail coats by those who could afford them – the gentlemen and perhaps some of the more successful *cearnach* – and there is some evidence for the use of padded akhetons and jacks. However, little – if any – use seems to have been made of defensive armour (excepting the targe) by the mid 17th century. This has been attributed to the introduction of the famous Highland Charge, but in reality such defensive armour would have proved no impediment to a brisk run of a hundred metres or so. The real reason for the abandonment or armour, as elsewhere in western Europe, was a simple recognition that mail coats and jacks provided absolutely no protection whatever against the firearms that were coming to dominate warfare.

Weapons and Tactics

In his report commissioned in 1724, General Wade set forth the classic description of Highland arms and tactics:

"The Arms they make use of in War, are, a Musket, a Broad Sword and Target, a Pistol and a Dirk or Dagger, hanging by their side, with a Powder Horn and a Pouch for their Ammunition. They form themselves into Bodies of unequal Numbers according to the strength of their Clan or Tribe, which is Commanded by their Respective Superior or Chieftain. When in sight of the Enemy they endeavour to possess themselves of

Highland Clansman identified by the Penicuik artist as Duncan MacGregor of Dalnasplutrach. Note how the targe is held up to cover his head.
[Author's collection]

the highest Ground, believing they descend on them with greater force.

"They generally give their fire at a distance, they lay down their Arms on the Ground and make a Vigorous attack with their Broad Swords, but if repulsed, seldom or never rally again. They dread engaging with the Cavalry and seldom venture to descend from the Mountains when apprehensive of being charged by them."

Somewhat in contradiction to this, and notwithstanding his obvious bias, General Hawley's rather more detailed description is equally useful. Unlike Wade, he had actually fought against the Jacobite Clans, at Sheriffmuir in 1715.

"They Commonly form their Front rank of what they call their best men, or True Highlanders, the number of which being allways but few, when they form in Battallions they commonly form four deep, & these Highlanders form the front of the four, the rest being lowlanders & arrant scum. When these battalions come within a large musket shott or three score yards [50m] this front rank gives their fire, and immediately throw down their firelocks and come down in a cluster with their swords and targets, making a noise and endeavouring to pierce the body or battalion before them – becoming twelve or fourteen deep by the time they come up to the people they attack."

Although Hawley's terminology might be a little unreliable, unlike Wade, he did correctly identify the way in which only the front rank of a Clan levy was made up of heavily armed gentlemen, while the two or three ranks standing behind comprised men who were neither trained nor equipped to be warriors. While the former were indeed generally armed in the manner described, and did lead their men forward, "with

Battle scene by the same artist. Once again the targes are held high. The original sketch shows them fighting against cavalrymen, though it is not known whether it was intended to represent an actual encounter, or recorded a training exercise against the Prince's Lifeguard. [Author's collection]

their swords and targets", the ordinary Clansmen who followed them were a different matter entirely.

The results of a military census carried out in five Perthshire parishes in 1638, on the eve of the Civil War, are particularly revealing. At first sight there appears to have been an abundance of swords, with only 11 out of 451 lacking one; on closer examination a very different picture emerges. Only 124 men, about a quarter of the total, conform to the accepted picture by carrying both sword and targe. This particular group was certainly well armed: no fewer than 92 of them also carried muskets and 65 had bows, including 54 of the musketeers (a somewhat unlikely combination, which is portrayed in one of the contemporary Stettin prints). Only 21 men carried sword and buckler alone.

By contrast, the remaining 315 swordsmen shared just five muskets and 73 bows between them. Clearly they were the forefathers of the "arrant scum", described by Hawley as standing behind the gentlemen, and as they do not carry targes, it is likely that all or most of the "swords" with which they are credited are actually dirks. These were substantial, usually single-edged, knives sharing certain characteristics with both the mediaeval ballock and rondel daggers. Having blades 15in or even 18in long, they might quite justifiably be classed as swords. In this context it is certainly significant that the Highlanders pictured at Stettin in 1631 carry long dirks in place of broadswords, and this practice was paralleled in Ireland. There the use of long-bladed swords was pretty largely confined to the chieftains and some professional soldiers, while the ordinary *kerns* are invariably described and depicted as being armed with *sgians* – long daggers similar to the dirk.

Out in the Hebrides things were evidently no better, and in 1689, when John Philip of Almerieclose described the largely Hebridean army assembled at Dalcomera in his epic poem *The Grameid*, he made very little mention of firearms. Swords are referred to rather more frequently in the poem, and sometimes targes, but the majority of the weapons

Rebellion Rewarded, a near contemporary propaganda piece purporting to depict the Jacobites at Carlisle. The piper on the left appears to be based on the well known print by Bowles, while the gent on the right bears a remarkable resemblance to Hogarth's portrait of Lord Lovat.
[Scottish National Portrait Gallery]

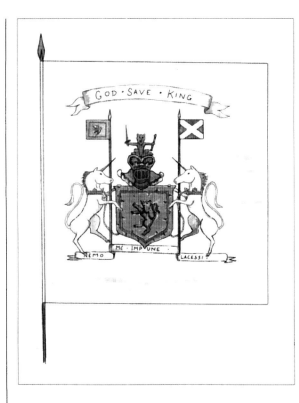

White silk colours with the Stewart's Arms *"God Save King"*. Probably carried by John Roy Stuart's Regiment. One of the three colours taken by Monro's 37th Foot at Culloden (*see Warrior 19*).

carried by the Clans at Dalcomera – and afterwards at Killiecrankie – were axes and spears.

Firearms

The rabble which won the battle of Prestonpans 50 years later were just as poorly armed: one hostile eyewitness in Edinburgh related how they carried scythes, pitchforks and a decidedly unimpressive selection of firearms, which included fowling pieces, old matchlocks and a number of broken and unserviceable pieces (**see commentary to Plate G**). The fact that, such useless weapons were being carried suggests that not withstanding the prominence given to fine broadswords in Gaelic literature, the prevailing view among the Clansmen was that real soldiers carried muskets. Interestingly enough, this same view was held by the Irish insurgents in Wexford in 1798, who were reported to be discarding good pikes in place of rusty and unserviceable firelocks. At any rate, the Highland army which drew up on Culloden Moor some months later was predominantly armed with French or Spanish firelocks and bayonets.

Nevertheless, there is little evidence that Clansmen made serious use of firearms. Traditionally, those who actually owned them carried their shot in their sporrans and powder in flasks. This was no doubt a useful enough mode of proceeding when hunting, but it placed Clansmen at a distinct disadvantage in a properly conducted firefight. This point was explicitly made by the Jacobite adjutant general, Colonel Sullivan, in rejecting a proposed defensive position reconnoitred by Lord George Murray near Culloden:

"Any man yt ever served with the highlanders, knows yt they fire but one shot & abandon their firelocks after. If there be any obstruction yt hinders them of going on the enemy all is lost; they don't like to be exposed to the enemy's fire, nor can they resist it, not being trained to charge [load] as fast as regular troops, especially the English wch are the troops in the world yt fires best."

The effectiveness of this one good volley is also questionable. Murray, deploring the fact that few Clansmen paused to deliver it at Culloden, complained: "This was a vast loss for the ffire of Highlanders is more bloody then that of any regular troups whatever." Generally speaking, subsequent writers have taken him at his word, but there is remarkably little evidence to back up his assertion.

Murray, it is true, may have been thinking of Falkirk, where a controlled volley delivered by the three MacDonald regiments at a range of ten yards broke up a cavalry charge. This was evidently exceptional, however, and both Wade and Hawley make the point that Highlanders normally fired at long range. Just as tellingly, no-one on the receiving end of a Highland charge ever seems to have complained of the volley which preceded it. At Prestonpans, for example, the onset was signalled by a "few dropping shots", but perhaps the most striking evidence comes from the celebrated encounter at High Bridge on 16 August 1745. Two additional, or depot, companies made up of recruits for the Royal Scots were ambushed there and after a long running battle forced to surrender a few hours later near Invergarry. When they did so, it was only because they were threatened with a full-scale attack on open ground by several hundred insurgents; up to that point they had only suffered two men killed and two more slightly wounded.

The fact of the matter is that most Clansmen were not intimately acquainted with firearms. While some were no doubt excellent shots, accustomed to deer stalking, there is a world of difference between taking a careful aimed shot at an unsuspecting stag and firing on a battlefield. Stewart of Garth makes this pertinent point in recollecting his own service in the West Indies. The Caribs had a considerable reputation as marksmen, and in order to test this he once asked a prisoner to hit an orange placed on a bottle 200 yards away. At the third attempt he did it. "I then asked him why he did not mark so well against the soldiers as against the orange; 'Massa,' he replied, 'the orange no gun or ball to shoot back; no run at me with bayonet.'"

Nevertheless, it seems fair to say that restricting themselves to a single, probably rather ragged, volley rather than attempt to establish fire superiority was the correct decision. Highland troops, including an alarming number of units which formed part of the 18th century British Army, almost invariably lacked the necessary training and discipline to engage in a firefight. Any attempt to do so, particularly against veterans, would have been futile. Instead they adopted the only other course open to them: they charged straight at the enemy.

Identified by the Penicuik artist as 'Glengarry', this is presumably Colonel Angus McDonnell, Glengarry's second son, who was accidentally shot and killed on 22 January 1746, when one of Clanranald's men failed to appreciate that the firelock he was cleaning was loaded. [Author's collection]

THE HIGHLAND CHARGE

It has been suggested that the Highland Charge was devised as late as 1642, by the celebrated Alasdair MacCholla, in order to better combine the use of firearms with cold steel. Up to a point this may be true, but the development may not have been as revolutionary as it first appears.

To begin with, it is necessary to appreciate the ordinary nature of Celtic/Heroic warfare. Those who were principally expected to do the fighting were the Highland gentlemen and the *caterans* – men who could afford the necessary weapons and, just as importantly, the time to practise with them. In time of conflict they would march forth behind their chieftain's banner, bringing with them their own followers – the ordinary Clansmen, collectively referred to as *ghillies*, comprising of tenants, sub-tenants and anybody else fit for it.

The task of these *ghillies* was threefold. They were first and foremost the outward symbol of their leader's power, but they also looked after the more mundane jobs on campaign, and in battle they backed their leader up.

At its most basic this back-up may have consisted of little more than forming an enthusiastic audience as he engaged in personal combat with a gentleman of the other party. However, in the early days at least, the *ghillies'* job during a pitched battle was evidently to provide fire support,

Highland sentinel after the Penicuik artist – note once again that he is armed only with a firelock and bayonet. [Author's collection]

sending showers of arrows over the advancing front line. A useful example of this can be seen at Auldearn, where Sir Mungo Campbell of Lawers' men were "shot" on to their objective by Seaforth's Mackenzies standing in their rear. Although they were no doubt then expected to back up their leaders once the charge proper began, their role does appear to have altered with the introduction of firearms.

While a bow can be used in both a direct and indirect 'fire' role, the same is not true of a musket, which is also much slower to reload. This had two important consequences. First, musket-armed gentlemen could only afford to fire once, at long range, before charging straight at the enemy sword in hand. Secondly, their followers would then no longer have been able to provide them with covering fire by shooting arrows over their heads, and so would have had little option than to physically back them up by participating in that charge. The net effect would have been to speed up the operation considerably and create the classic Highland Charge.

The Highland Charge is perhaps best illustrated by looking at two notable Jacobite successes, Killiecrankie and Prestonpans, and contrasting them with one even more notable failure, Culloden.

Killiecrankie

At Killiecrankie a regular army led by a Highlander, Hugh Mackay of Scourie, encountered a Highland army led by a Lowlander, John Graham, Viscount Dundee, just north of the Pass of Killiecrankie on 27 July 1689. Neither army had initially expected a battle, and by hard marching Mackay was able to secure the pass and bring his army through it unmolested. Too late to ambush him, the Highlanders instead deployed high on the slopes of Creag Eallaich, overlooking the road, but Mackay turned to face them and drew his army up on the Urrard Plateau, a fairly level shelf of ground halfway up the hill.

Having only two small troops of volunteer cavalry, Mackay was understandably concerned about his flanks. His left wing was secured by posting a detachment of grenadiers commanded by Lieutenant Colonel Lauder on "a little hill wreathed with trees", while the right was similarly anchored on a stream near the entrance to the pass. To link these positions he ordered his 3,500 infantry to double their files – to draw up three deep instead of the customary six. Afterwards Mackay was much criticised for this, but in fact it allowed him to deploy more musketeers in the firing line and so improve his chances of stopping the Highland attack dead in its tracks. Unfortunately, for some unknown reason, Lord Kenmore's Regiment, standing in the very centre of the line, remained standing in six ranks. As a result, while there was the usual interval of about 50m between most of Mackay's regiments, there existed a gap of about 100m between Kenmore's men and the nearest battalion on their left; thanks to some boggy ground, no less than 150m separated them

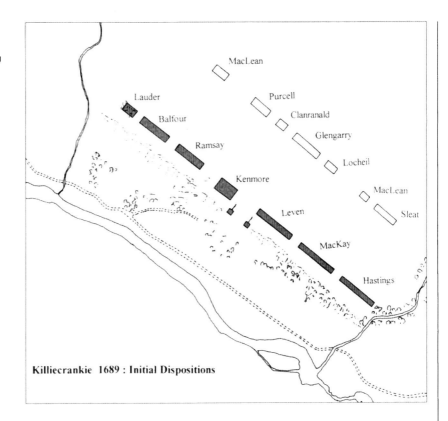

MacLean

Purcell

Lauder

Clanranald

Balfour

Glengarry

Ramsay

Locheil

Kenmore

MacLean

Leven

Sleat

MacKay

Hastings

Killiecrankie 1689 : Initial Dispositions

from Leven's Regiment on their right. To all intents and purposes, Kenmore's newly raised regiment, perhaps the least reliable unit in Mackay's army, was left on its own, isolated in the very centre of the line.

Further up the hill, Dundee had come to the uncomfortable realisation that his 2,500 men were badly outnumbered. This disparity was made all the more apparent when Mackay extended his front. In order to cover it, Dundee was obliged to disperse his forces with substantial gaps between his regiments (**see above map**) and as a result the Highland Charge actually took the form of three poorly co-ordinated attacks at different points along Mackay's front at about 8 o'clock in the evening.

Most of Dundee's regiments were massed in the centre, with the object of piercing Mackay's centre, but Locheil's Camerons, instead of joining Glengarry's men in attacking Leven's Regiment, veered off to their left and joined with Sir Alexander MacLean's and Sleat's men in attacking Mackay's own regiment. This had some interesting consequences. In the first place it exposed Locheil's men to a murderous flanking fire as they crossed Leven's front. According to some accounts they lost as many as 120 men out of 300. If so, they must effectively have been destroyed as a military unit. Hoping to profit from this disaster, Mackay tried to counter-attack with his two cavalry troops, but he was in turn charged by Dundee's cavalry and driven back on Kenmore's Regiment. Thus ridden over by

21

Traditionally identified as Donald Cameron of Locheil, this sitter actually appears to be his son, James Cameron of Locheil. If so, the painting shows the uniform of an officer of the *Royal Ecossois* – a blue jacket with red velvet collar and cuffs, silver braid and the silver epaulette introduced for commissioned ranks in the early 1760s. The plaid is predominantly red and black.

[Private Scottish collection]

their own cavalry, Kenmore's men, who were already feeling rather lonely, were in no condition to resist as the Clansmen forming the Jacobite centre swept down on them. Both they and the left division of Leven's Regiment simply threw down their arms and ran away.

Meanwhile, further to their right, the MacLeans had fallen on Mackay's Regiment, overrunning its right division but ignoring both Hastings' Regiment on the extreme right and the remainder of Mackay's and Leven's regiments. The latter oversight was particularly unfortunate since it was a volley from one of these units which killed Dundee, the Jacobite commander.

To the left of Kenmore's unfortunate regiment, the three battalions commanded by Brigadier Balfour were at first barely menaced by Sir John MacLean's solitary regiment. But owing to the curvature of the hill, Balfour was unable to see beyond the massive hole torn in Mackay's centre. Unaware that elements of the right wing were still holding their ground, he assumed that everyone to his right had given way and so began to execute an orderly withdrawal towards the River Garry. However, as soon as his men began to descend the steep, tree-covered slope at the edge of the plateau, they were simultaneously attacked in front by MacLean's men and in flank by a contingent of Athollmen coming down the valley from Blair. Panicking, all three battalions broke without fighting and suffered terrible losses as they fled towards the river.

This left only Hastings' Regiment (the only English unit to take part in the battle) and the battered remains of Leven's and Mackay's regiments, now commanded by the general himself. Still full of fight, they took up a defensive position around Urrard House, but to their surprise were left unmolested. When darkness fell they were able to execute an orderly withdrawal across the river and link up with the survivors of Balfour's command.

Prestonpans

At Prestonpans the two sides fielded about the same number of men, but a substantial proportion of General Sir John Cope's regulars were cavalry. At dawn on 21 September 1745 the Highland Army charged across a flat stubble-covered field and in a matter of minutes swept Cope's army out of existence. Once again, however, a close examination of the evidence reveals an interesting sequence of events.

Cope's army was occupying a flat, open field, protected on two sides by buildings and enclosures and on a third by a marsh which prevented a direct assault by the Highland Army. In the end, a night march brought the Highlanders round to the open east side by dawn on the morning of the 21st, but in order to deploy they first had to march across Cope's front. When the Highlanders were set upon by a dragoon picquet, he ordered his men to stand to their arms and wheel to the left in order to face the imminent threat.

In the race to form in line of battle before Cope's men, the Duke of Perth, commanding the leading Jacobite division, led his men too far northwards. Sufficient room was to have been left between this division and the marsh to allow the second division, commanded by Lord George Murray, to deploy on their left. However, in the poor light Perth mis-judged the difference and when he eventually halted and turned to face the British Army, a huge gap had opened up between the two divisions.

This accident had quite unforeseen consequences. Cope had by now deployed his army in conventional fashion, with one of his two dragoon regiments on each flank of his infantry. They should have comprised two-and-a-half battalions of regulars, but in the hurry to form up, the substantial detachments forming the outlying picquets had simply fallen in on the right of the line, making up a small ad hoc battalion of their own. As the Highland attack came in, Perth's division found itself facing Hamilton's 14th Dragoons and Murray's men fell on Gardiner's 13th Dragoons and the picquets. The greater part of Cope's infantry had no enemy at all to their immediate front.

Both dragoon regiments were already in a rather shaky condition, and on receiving a few "scattering shots" promptly ran off. The picquets, lacking officers and with little cohesion, also gave way, leaving both flanks of the infantry exposed. At this point most of the Highlanders simply carried straight on in pursuit of the fugitives, and Murray afterwards recorded his surprise at realising the rest of the regulars were still standing formed behind him. In a matter of minutes, however, they too were dealt with as the open flanks were rolled up. Perhaps the best description of this came from Major Severne of Lascelles' 58th Foot, who testified at the subsequent inquiry that, ". . . a large body of their Left rush'd on obliquely on our Right Flank, and broke the Foot as it were by Platoons, with so rapid a Motion, that the whole Line was broken in a few Minutes". Indeed, although he was understandably rather defensive about the fact, Colonel Lascelles himself was able to make good his escape by running off to the east through the still substantial gap that

18th century military shoes as worn by Highland regiments. The buckles were excavated at Fort Ticonderoga.
[Author's collection]

existed between the stragglers of the two victorious Jacobite divisions.

At Killiecrankie and Prestonpans, therefore, it is clear that the popular impression of the hapless Redcoats being literally swept away by an "avalanche of steel" is a gross over-simplification. In both cases, gaps opened up in the defending line when one or more units panicked and ran *before* the Highlanders actually made contact. The Clansmen then poured into these gaps, and while a substantial number rushed straight into the enemy rear, with the object of cutting down fugitives and getting in among the baggage train, others rolled up the open flanks of those regular units still holding their ground.

It is important to emphasise that cases of Highlanders physically tackling formed infantry units head-on and literally battering or even carving their way through are virtually non-existent. At Alford in 1645, for example, the defeated General Baillie declared: "Our foot stood with myselfe and behaved themselves as became them, untill the enemies horse charged in our reare, and in front we were overcharged with their foot." Similarly, at Falkirk, after beating off a cavalry attack, the Highland Army charged General Hawley's infantry. Struggling up a rough hillside with a storm beating in their faces, the left wing regiments made no attempt to stand, but ran away at once, before the Jacobites actually came into contact. What should have been a stunning Rebel victory was then thrown away as most of the Highlanders set off enthusiastically in pursuit, keeping well clear of the regiments on Hawley's right who not only stood their ground but eventually mounted a dangerous counter-attack before retiring in good order to their camp.

Culloden

Although it was to be the Highland Clans' last and most famous defeat, the battle of Culloden provides what is perhaps the clearest picture of

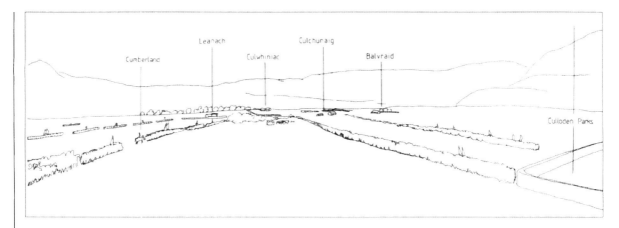

their tactics. The Jacobite Army drew up on an open stretch of common grazing land, apparently well suited for the Highland Charge – criticism that it was *too* open ignores the point that the Clansmen needed open ground in order to launch their charge – at Prestonpans they had chosen to attack across an even flatter field.

Unlike previous battles, they were for the first time exposed to well handled artillery at Culloden, and for that very reason began the attack within a few minutes of coming under fire. Ordinarily the rebel line might have been expected to advance fairly steadily until within musket shot of the British front line, fire, and then rush in under their own

Panorama of Culloden based on a watercolour sketch by Thomas Sandby.
[Author's collection]

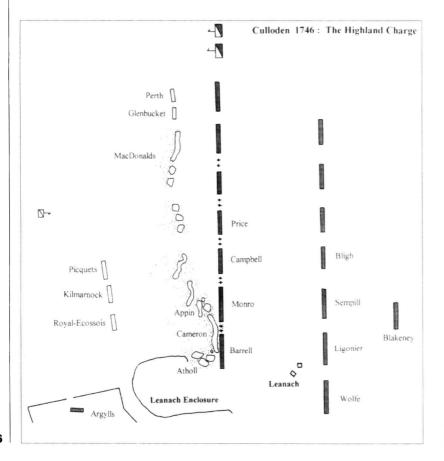

Culloden 1746 : The Highland Charge

Culloden Moor detail.
[Author's collection]

Another trophy of Culloden: Piece of blue silk with a St. Andrew saltire "*Commit the Work to God*".
[Author's collection]

smoke. However, in an obvious effort to minimise the time spent under artillery fire, they instead surged forward at a run. Many of the front rank men even threw away their firelocks and drew their swords at the outset. A number of eyewitnesses in the British ranks afterwards testified that as they came forward, they coalesced into three distinct bodies, or wedges, and it is instructive to examine the fortunes of each in turn.

The left wing, mainly comprising MacDonald regiments, had furthest to go and, crucially, was not coming under much artillery fire. It advanced to within musket-shot of the British front line and there came to a halt. What happened next is clearly described in the victorious Duke of Cumberland's own dispatch: "They came running on in their wild manner . . . they came down three several Times with a Hundred Yards of our Men, firing their pistols and brandishing their Swords, but the Royals and Pulteneys hardly took their Firelocks from their shoulders . . . "

In other words, they were making short, vicious rushes, hoping to stampede one or more of the regiments opposing them. All, however, stood firm and in the end it was the Highlanders who fell back, menaced by Cumberland's cavalry.

At the other end of the line, the Jacobite right wing could not afford to waste time with feints, and for once, battered by both artillery and musketry, went straight in and attempted to physically break Barrell's 4th Foot. The regulars, refusing to be intimidated, met them with charged bayonets, and hand-to-hand fighting ensued before sheer weight of numbers prevailed and the Highlanders broke through. Ordinarily such a penetration, especially on the flank would have then seen some Highlanders exploiting towards the rear and spreading all manner of fear, confusion and despondency, while others rolled up the flank thereby exposed. Indeed, at this point it is significant that the central Jacobite column, instead of attempting to engage the regiments standing directly opposite, actually veered across their front instead (getting badly shot up in the process – as Locheil's had been at Killiecrankie) in order to follow the right column into the gap torn in the British line.

Unfortunately, as Barrell's burst apart under the pressure, the next battalion in line, Monro's 37th, managed to refuse its left flank and thus prevent the Highlanders from rolling up the line, while at the same time General Huske counter-attacked with four battalions from the British second line, sealing off the penetration and flaying the Highlanders with a deadly crossfire.

While the battle was exceptional in that artillery fire forced the Clansmen in the right and centre divisions to come charging straight in, it otherwise provides an excellent demonstration of Highland tactics. Untroubled by artillery fire, the MacDonalds were able to make three attempts to shake the enemy. Failing to do so, they made no serious attempt to close and eventually made off without pressing home their attack. It is not entirely true to describe the Highland Charge as a 'one

ABOVE **Partly reconstructed Culwhiniac Park wall looking towards the Jacobite start-line, just in front of the farm buildings at Culchunaig – in the heavy clump of trees on the skyline. [Author's collection]**

LEFT **View from Culwhiniac Park across the Leanach enclosure to the British Army's front line. The National Trust for Scotland is reconstructing the walls after locating their original position through geophysical survey. [Author's collection]**

Although the Jacobites suc-ceeded in breaking through the British front line, they were immediately hit by a four-bat-talion counter-attack led by Daddy Huske, which sealed off the penetration. One of Sandby's sketches shows that Ligonier's Regiment had to divide into two wings in order to clear the Leanach steading – which afterwards appears to have served as a British Army field hospital.
[Author's collection]

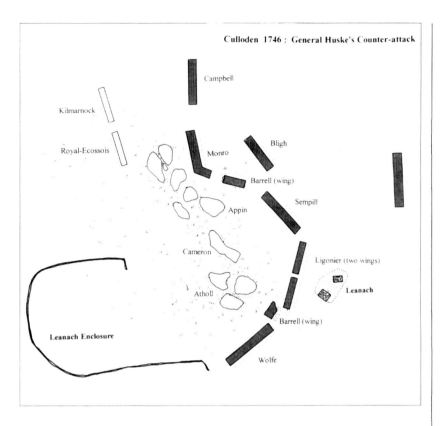

Culloden 1746 : General Huske's Counter-attack

shot' weapon: such feints could be carried out almost indefinitely. At Sheriffmuir in 1715 the Highland left is said to have tried to come forward no fewer than 12 times before eventually retreating across the Allan Water. Once they did advance to contact, however, they were indeed committed for good or ill.

On the Jacobite right at Culloden, the charge went home, but because the enemy had not been intimidated, and did not run away, the Clansmen were unable to exploit this localised success in the usual manner. However, unaware of this, the central division tried to reinforce the apparent success instead of attempting their own breakthrough and found themselves in a death-trap.

The problem with the Highland Charge was that given the right con-ditions – a collapse of a part of the line facing them, creating a breach which could be exploited – it could bring spectacular success. But if the enemy was not obliging enough to give way to panic, the Clansmen lacked the discipline, technology and sheer staying power to create that breach by more direct means. What's more, they were themselves extremely vulnerable to counter-attacks as was seen to dramatic effect when Huske's regiments in the reserve came forward to close off any penetration in the first line. Ironically enough, it was only after his assim-ilation into the British Army after 1745 that the Highland Clansman was able to achieve his full military potential.

THE PLATES

A: ON THE MARCH

This bucolic scene is substantially based upon a useful account by an English officer named Captain Edward Burt, who assisted in General Wade's celebrated road-making in the 1730s: "When a chief goes a journey in the Hills, or makes a formal visit to an equal, he is said to be attended by all or the most part of the officers following, viz. *The Hanchman*: This officer is a sort of secretary and is to be ready upon all occasions to venture his life in defence of his master; and at drinking bouts he stands behind his seat, at his haunch (from whence his title is derived) and watches the conversation, to see if any one offends his patron. *Bard*: his poet. *Bladier*: his spokesman. *Gilli-more*: carries his broadsword. *Gilli-casflue*: carries him when on foot, over the fords. *Gilly comstrainie*: leads his horse in rough and dangerous ways. *Gilly-trushanarnish*: the baggage man. *The Piper*: who being a gentleman, I should have named him sooner. *The Piper's Gilly*: who carries the bagpipe. There are likewise some gentlemen, near of kin, who bear him company; and besides, a number of the common sort, who have no particular employment, but follow him only to partake of the cheer."

Good cheer generally seems to have been available in considerable abundance. Duncan Forbes of Culloden was particularly noted for his hospitality (running his own distillery at Ferintosh obviously helped) and it was said of him: "Few go away sober at any time; and for the greatest part of his guests . . . they cannot go away at all."

As to the individuals depicted here, all were neighbours of Culloden and undoubtedly sampled his famous hospitality at one time or another. **1** The chief, perched on a small Highland pony or Garron, is based on a portrait of Major James Fraser of Castle Leathers. **2** The genial host is based on James Moray of Abercairney, as painted by Jeremiah Davidson in about 1735. **3** The henchman and **4** piper are based on Richard Waitt's portraits of Alastair Mor Grant of Stratham and William Cumming, Champion and Piper to the Laird of Grant respectively. Alastair Mor has one of the curved sabres, known as *turcaich*, or turks. William Cumming is said to have died as the result of a wager between Grant and the Laird of Mackintosh as to which of them had the lustiest piper. Both pipers set out from Mackintosh's seat at Moy, playing for all they were worth, but only Cumming succeeded in reaching Castle Grant, and reputedly expired after collapsing in the hall.

The two men wear what is presumably a livery tartan that differs only in minor detail: Alastair Mor's plaid is bound with yellow tape and Cumming's is bound with red. The latter's jacket and waistcoat are also in the Grant livery colours of red and green.

B: HIGHLAND GENTLEMAN 1680

This splendid figure, largely based on John Michael Wright's portrait of Sir Mungo Murray (1668-1700), displays all the finery, and the variety of weapons and equipment generally associated with the Highland gentleman or *duine wasal* of the period studied here.

Of particular interest is the form of bandoleer he wears for

John Gordon of Glenbucket (c.1674-1750), a veteran Jacobite officer who reputedly gave King George II nightmares. This portrait appears to have been 'improved' in Victorian times, but the likeness is in accordance both with contemporary descriptions and a sketch by the Penicuik artist. [Author's collection]

carrying individual charges of powder – for his pistol rather than for the firelock, to judge by their size. In September 1678 two of the Independent Companies raised for policing the Highlands were between them issued with 300 firelocks and bayonets and 300 bandoleers, presumably of a more substantial type than worn by Murray himself. The collar of bandoleers depicted in detail (**1**) is a Scottish one, since it has 16 bandoleers or individual chargers attached to the leather collar. Official ammunition scales were remarkably consistent throughout the 17th century: each soldier was allowed one pound (454g) of powder and one pound of ball. Since the Scots Privy Council ordered in 1666 that all muskets should be of "16 Balles" (a bore suitable for musket balls weighing one ounce, or one sixteenth of a pound – hence 16 bore), 16 charges of powder were required to fire off those 16 balls, and 16 bandoleers in which to contain them.

2 The firelock depicted here (dated 1685) is a typical example of a 17th century Scottish fowling piece with a *snaphaunce* mechanism, although an English *Dog-Lock* mechanism is also shown in detail (**3**). Firelocks of the latter type appear to have only been issued to men of the Independent companies.

Braemar Castle, a typical example of an "L Plan" tower house forming a chief's residence. The Jacobite standard was raised outside in 1715. [Author's collection]

Other items issued to the companies included two pairs of colours, four drums and four blunderbusses (whether these were to be carried by the drummers is not apparent, but at the very least it is an intriguing possibility), 1,500 flints, four pairs of bullet moulds, each capable of casting a dozen bullets at once, two more for casting shot for the blunderbusses, and a pair of shears for clipping the newly cast balls. In addition, the barracks ordered to be built for their accommodation at Inverlochy was to be supplied with "forty axes, twenty mattocks, brewing loomes [tubs] for thrie bols at a tyme, two iron potts, fifty payr of bedplayds, 150 wooden playtts, 300 horn spoones, fourscore two [82] pynt stoopes, ten duzon [120] of timber trencheours, four score tupp horns for drinking".

Swords, dirks and targes were not issued, presumably because the Highland gentlemen who enlisted in the companies brought their own. The dirk shown here (**4**) is an unusual 17th century variant with a cast brass hilt in place of the more common intricately carved bog oak grip. Although typically 17th century in style, the broadsword hilt – copied from Murray's portrait – is extremely unusual in that it appears to be gilded.

5 Many Highland targes or shields were simple affairs comprising two layers of wood pegged and glued together with a covering of cowhide and a deerhide lining. Some form of padding was inserted between the two layers of wood – raw wool, moss or anything else which came to hand. A targe of this style, said to have been carried by a Grant of Glenmoriston in 1719, is illustrated, together with the more elaborate one described in a letter written by one Henry Fletcher, brother to the famous Laird of Saltoun, in 1716:

6 "The outward forme of ane Highland Targe is a convex circle, about 2 foot in diameter, but some have them oval; the innermost part of it nixt the man's breast is a skin with the hair upon it, which is only a cover to a steel plate [**a**], which is not very thick, for the whole is no great weight; on the inner side of this Steel plate the Handle is fixed, which hath two parts, one that the left arm passes throw till near the elbow, the other that the Hand lays on: without the Steel plate there is a cork [**c**] which covers the Steel plate exactly, but betwixt the Cork and the Steel plate there is Wooll [**b**] stuffed in very hard: the Cork is covered with plain well-wrought leather [**d**], which is nailed to the cork with nails that have brass heads, in order round, drawing thicker towards the centre. From the centre sticks out a Stiletto [**7**] (I know not the right name of it, but I call it so, because it is a sort of short poignard) which fixes into the steel plate and wounds the Enemy when they close: about this Stiletto [**a**] closs to the Targe there is a peece of Brass in the form of a Cupelo [**c**] about 3 inches over and coming half way out on the stiletto and is fixed upon it. Within this brass there is a peece of Horn [**b**] of the same forme like a cup, out of which they drink their usquebaugh, but it being pierced in the under part by the Stiletto, when they take it off to use it as a cup, they are obliged to apply the forepart of the end of their finger to the hole to stop it, so that they might drink out of their cup."

Charles Edward Stuart (1720-88), leader of the last and most disastrous of all the Jacobite risings. This portrait is the only one known to have been executed while he was in Scotland. The artist, Robert Strange, served in his Lifeguards. [Scottish National Portrait Gallery]

The small cup is a form of quaich, used for the drinking of spirits and more often than not for the pledging of health. A more typical example (**8**), with its distinctive 'wings', is also illustrated, together with some rather more mundane horn beakers (**9**), and a staved wooden stoup of the kind issued to the Inverlochy garrison (**10**).

C: RECRUITING FOR THE PRINCE'S ARMY, 1745

The news that Charles Edward Stuart had raised his father's standard at Glenfinnan set in train an intensive recruitment drive. In theory the process was simple enough: once a chief had decided to commit himself, he summoned his immediate relations – "gentlemen near of kin" – to a traditional rendezvous point; each in turn brought his own personal following. There was likely to be little argument since military service was an accepted obligation, but difficulties did arise if a laird was absent or too far away to exert proper control over his tenants or offer them his protection from other recruiters.

Glen Urquhart provides a useful case in point. All those living there were directly or indirectly tenants of the Laird of Grant, who veered between neutrality and support for the Government. On the whole he was successful in keeping his Speyside tenants out of the rising, but, as so often before, the Glen Urquhart tenants – out of reach on the other side of Loch Ness – went their own way. At a meeting in the kirkyard most were talked into supporting the Pretender and ended up in Glengarry's Regiment.

Such meetings were rare and a great many others were given little or no choice in the matter. A considerable number of the men brought to trial after the rising testified that they had been forced out either by threats that their homes would be burnt and their cattle taken, or indeed because they were simply beaten up, and not always by their own superiors.

Typical evidence of this came from a chronicler of the rebellion in Aberdeenshire, who remarked that Lord Lewis Gordon's threats of burning "soon had the desired effect, for the burning of a single house or farm stack in a Parish terrified the whole, so that they would quickly send in their proportion [of recruits] and by this means, with the few that joined as volunteers, he raised near 300 men called the Strathboggy Battalion in the country thereabouts".

More dramatically, perhaps, the Loyalist James Robertson, Minister of Lochbroom in Ross-shire, described how MacDonnell of Keppoch and some of his people turned up there on 17 March 1746 and "unexpectedly surprized the poor people, snatching some of them out of their beds. Others, who thought their old age would excuse them, were dragged from their ploughs . . . while some were taken off the highways. One I did myself see overtaken by speed of foot, and when he declared he would rather die than be carried to the rebellion, was knock'd to the ground by the butt of a musket and carried away all bleed."

It is very hard to escape the impression that the reason why so many old men are found among the hundreds of Jacobite prisoners is because they were simply unable to outrun the recruiting parties. One Rebel officer, Captain John MacLean, blithely recorded in his diary: ". . . the Landlord William McGlashen Went off with me in the Morning the 16 Septr and two men more, and we Catched a Deserter in a moor in Our Way but after two or three miles travelling with us we let him Goe he being 70 years old, only took his Sword for one of our men."

Coercion of this kind was not confined to the Rebel army, or for that matter to the desperate days of the rising. A possibly apocryphal story tells how a visitor to Perthshire in the 1790s saw a young man being enthusiastically pursued by some of the Duke of Atholl's servants. On enquiring what terrible crime the fugitive had committed, he was cheerfully assured that far from being a criminal, the young man was merely in the process of being recruited into the Atholl *volunteers*!

This party, based upon contemporary sketches of Jacobite soldiers by the Penicuik artist, is raising 'volunteers' for one of the two Fraser battalions. The colour, which bears the arms of Lieutenant-Colonel Charles Fraser of Inverallochie, was among those captured at Culloden.

D: FIREARMS

Highland, or rather Scottish, firearms were distinctive in form. Most notable were the all-metal pistols, made chiefly at Doune, which had cast steel (or less commonly brass) stocks in place of the conventional wooden ones. This permitted a considerable variety of styles and decoration, particularly engraving and inlay.

Another characteristic was the widespread use of the snaphaunce lock – thought to reflect Dutch influence – during the 17th century. This was an early form of flintlock featuring a quite separate pan cover and frizzen. Unlike the more familiar 'French' lock, which gradually superseded it in the

On the March

A

Highland Gentleman 1680 (See text commentary for detailed captions)

B

Recruiting for the Prince's Army, 1745

C

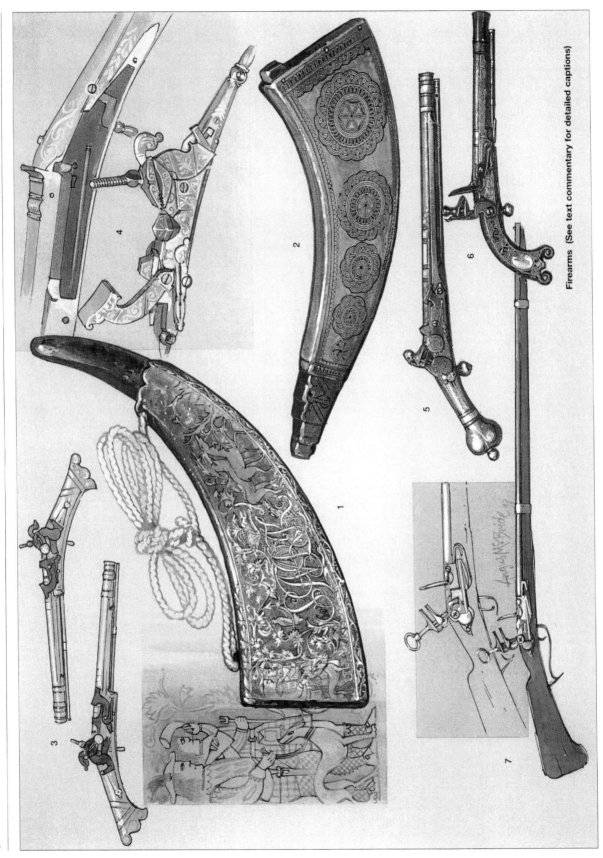

Firearms (See text commentary for detailed captions)

D

Lord Lewis Gordon and his Master Burner, 1646

E

Highland Clansman 1745
(See text commentary for detailed captions)

F

At Rest – the Potterow Port, Edinburgh, 1745

G

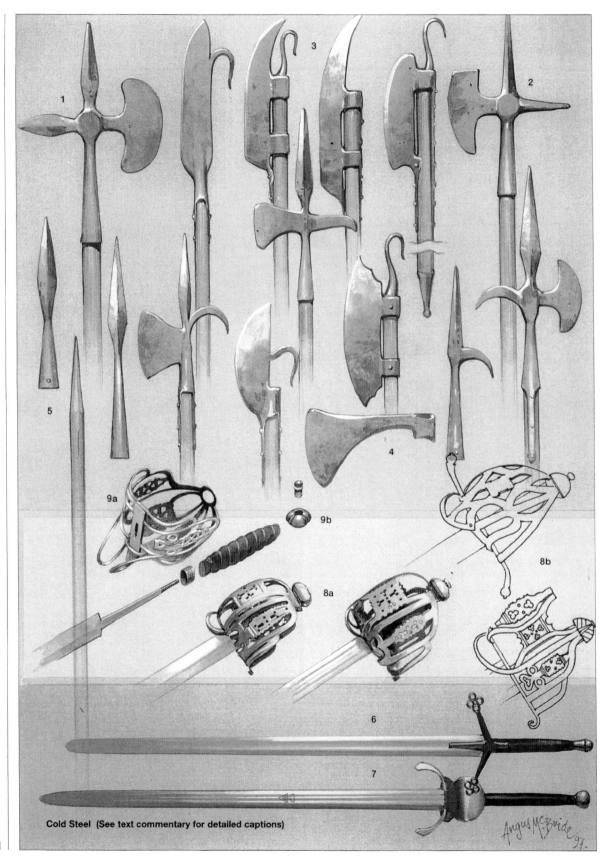

1 2 3 5 4 9a 9b 8b 8a 6 7

Cold Steel (See text commentary for detailed captions)

Angus McBride '97.

H

Battle (1) Auldearn 1645

Battle (2) Culloden 1746

J

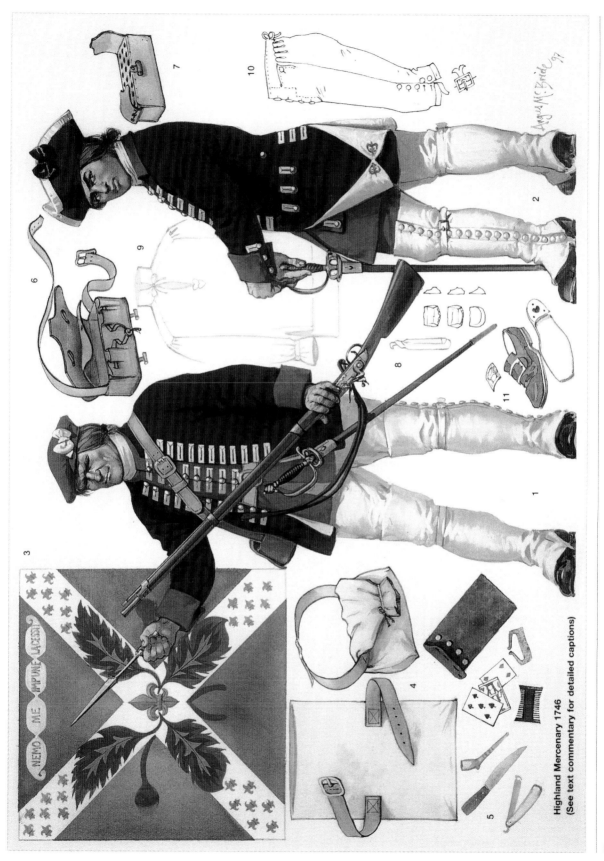

Highland Mercenary 1746
(See text commentary for detailed captions)

K

Afterwards: Duchess Jean recruiting for the Gordons 1794

A useful engraving by Van Gucht depicting a private and corporal of an early Highland regiment. [Author's collection]

Clansman identified by the Penicuik artist as "Shiterluck Younger" – presumably the McGhie of Shirloch mortally wounded and captured at Culloden while serving with the Atholl Brigade. [Author's collection]

18th century, it required the pan cover to be opened manually before pulling the trigger. For some reason Scottish gun-smiths also showed a marked reluctance to fit trigger-guards to their pieces.

Scottish-made muskets, on the other hand, generally had wooden stocks carved in the distinctive style (shown in **Plate B**) though all-metal examples do exist. They were otherwise similar to the pistols, and featured snaphaunce locks and unguarded triggers. This style appears to be principally associated with the 17th century. However, a firelock of this type

RIGHT **Highland troops on the march c.1743. Although this series of strip cartoons depicts officers, men and dogs of the 43rd Highlanders making their way through Germany, Clan regiments would no doubt have straggled in a similar fashion. Note the various ways of wearing the plaid and the fact that a number of men are still carrying targes.**
46 | [National Museums of Scotland]

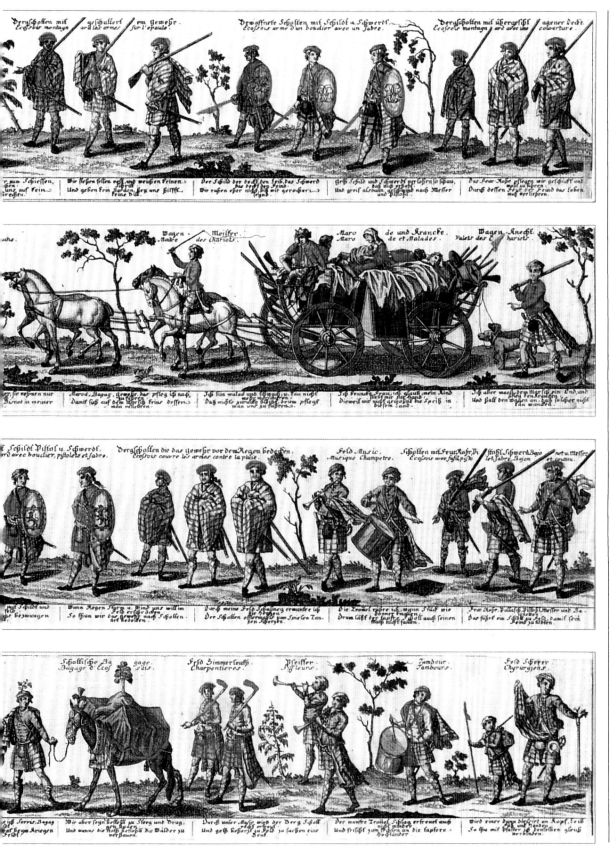

47

Lord Lewis Gordon (1725-54). A renegade naval officer, he raised a three-battalion regiment in the north-east of Scotland which protected the Jacobite left flank at Culloden. [Private collection]

animals, although very common in America, are quite rare in Scotland. In this particular case the horn provides extreme;y valuable evidence on the construction of trews. Note the dagged seams at the rear, and the separately cut legs. Items shown are as follows; **1** 17th century powderhorn with hunting scene; **2** powderhorn with traditional celtic designs c.1690; **3** a pair of all-brass snaphaunce pistols; **4** snaphaunce lock 1613 – note that the pistol stock is hollow; **5** steel and silver snaphaunce pistol 1672; **6** classic styled "Doune" pistol c.1740, and (**7**) a Spanish "Escopeta" c.1719.

E: LORD LEWIS GORDON AND HIS MASTER BURNER, 1646

Highland troops traditionally excelled in raiding and in running off cattle. On the night of 27 October 1745, for example, a party of Frasers, thwarted in their aim of seizing the house and person of the Lord President, Duncan Forbes of Culloden (they had been seen off by a swivel gun shrewdly fired from his bedroom window), consoled themselves by lifting his cattle instead. Although these affairs could sometimes be high spirited and exciting enough, in reality they were all too often little more than squalid combinations of armed robbery and naked terrorism.

Far more typical, perhaps, were the operations of Lord Lewis Gordon in Morayshire in the early months of 1646. As the Civil War in Scotland entered its final year, the dwindling Royalist armies fought with increasing desperation. Although the great Montrose had been broken at Philiphaugh in the previous summer and was now engaged in a pointless siege of Inverness, George Gordon, Marquis of Huntly, had

does appear in Waitt's portrait of Alasdair Mor Grant of Stratham, possibly c.1714, and, Patrick Crichton of Woodhouselee mentions ın his account of the Jacobite occupation of Edinburgh in 1745 that some Highlanders had firelocks with butts "turned up lick a heren [herring]" – probably a fairly good layman's description of this style. Generally speaking however, Scottish gun-makers tended to specialise in pistols, which meant that, particularly in the 18th century, most 'shoulder' guns were imported into the highlands, clandestinely or otherwise.

In his report on the Highlands compiled in 1724, General Wade noted: "The Spaniards who landed at Castle Donnan in the Year 1719 brought with them a great Number of Arms: They were delivered to the Rebellious Highlanders who are still possessed of them, many of which I have seen in my passage through that Country, and I judge them to be the same from their peculiar make and the fashion of their Locks."

The Spanish firelock which Wade was referring to was the *Escopeta*, which does indeed feature a very distinctive *Catalan* stock and *Miquelet* lock. A number of these weapons, picked up during or after the '45, were for a time displayed in the Tower of London before being lost in the great fire of October 1841, and are featured in a number of McIan's reconstructions.

Considerable use was made of powderhorns, which were almost invariably flattened, after being softened up in boiling water. As a rule, decoration tended to be quite formal, and examples such as the one shown here featuring men and

Clansman with *Turceach*, or Turkish-style, bladed broadsword. [Author's collection]

returned from exile in the far north, raised a rag-tag army and commenced clearing out the numerous small Government-held posts in Morayshire. Some fell quickly, but while he was tied up in a prolonged siege of Letham Castle, near Auldearn, his younger son, Lord Lewis Gordon, occupied Rothes in order to mark young Grant of Ballindalloch's garrison in Spynie.

Hampered by the bitter winter weather, no attempt was made by either party to mount a serious assault on the other. Instead, the two men played the part of robber barons, periodically issuing out of their strongholds to plunder and burn the surrounding villages. Lord Lewis Gordon and his Highlanders were, according to all contemporary chroniclers, easily the wildest and the worst scourge of the hapless local population. Indeed, according to one of them, James Fraser, Gordon even employed in his train a master burner, who "upon the sign given to him would instantly set fire to the cornstacks, and put all in a flame".

Appropriately, this particular dawn raid in part follows contemporary etchings of marauders at work during the Thirty Years War, while Gordon's Highlanders are themselves for the most part based on the well known Stettin prints, depicting Highland mercenaries serving in Germany at the time.

F: HIGHLAND CLANSMAN 1745

By the middle of the 18th century the plain coloured doublets seen earlier – blue ones were particularly popular – had given way to tartan jackets and sometimes tartan waistcoats as well, in a set which normally complemented but did not match the plaid. In ordinary life the knitted blue bonnet was worn without adornment, but Jacobite troops identified themselves by attaching white cockades, as shown here, sometimes adding an interesting copper badge intended to be sewn either to a bonnet or, more usually, a jacket. The white cockade is sometimes romantically linked with the white rose, but in point of fact it was a simple form of field sign which contrasted with the black ones already worn by British military units. Highland Loyalist units found through experience that black cockades were inadequate for identification purposes, so they supplemented them with the much more visible red crosses worn by the earlier Independent Companies. This was considered much more practical than the suggestion made after Falkirk that they should be issued with soldiers' hats for recognition.

While the archetypal Highland gentleman (**profiled in Plate B**) generally strode forth as heavily armed as any Balkan warlord, the ordinary Clansman following his banner was normally much less burdened with warlike implements. On 6 December 1745 a Jacobite officer named Lord Lewis Gordon (a descendant of the man who employed the master burner) instructed his officers that: "All men are to be well cloathed, with short cloathes, plaid, new shoes and three pair of hose and accoutered with shoulder ball gun [as distinct from a fowling piece or shotgun], pistolls and sword." Although this was clearly the ideal, it appears that it was rarely achieved in practice. While swords were certainly prized as status symbols and carried wherever possible, contemporary illustrations (particularly the Penicuik sketches) and documentary evidence demonstrate that most ordinary Jacobite soldiers – and their Loyalist counterparts in the Independent Companies – were armed only with firelocks and bayonets.

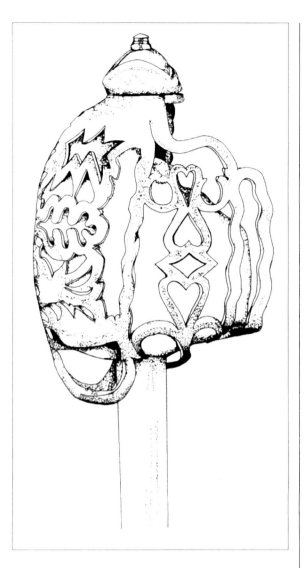

A typical example of the very florid 'Stirling'-style broadsword hilt. [Author's collection]

On 15 May 1746 a party of 77 men belonging to Glengarry's Regiment surrendered 65 firelocks, 26 swords and four dirks, while 98 of Keppoch's Regiment handed in a firelock apiece but only 22 swords and one dirk. Two days later, on 17 May, another party, this time of 44 men, surrendered 27 firelocks, three swords and six pistols. Similar figures were reported from other groups laying down their arms at that time, and only in one instance, a party of 23 Clan Chattan men who also surrendered on the 17th, was there anything even approaching parity in the numbers of firelocks and swords given up – 16 firelocks and 13 swords. It may, of course, be argued that it was easy enough to conceal a family dirk or even the pistols (which are so prominent by their absence), but the lack of swords is a different matter. No doubt some were hidden away rather than given up, but the figures for the *materiel* actually recovered by the British Army from Culloden Moor indicate that the proportion of swords held back cannot have been very high.

On the day of the battle Cumberland optimistically reckoned that the Rebel army had lost nearly 2,000 dead, wounded and prisoners. Hardly surprisingly then. 2,320 firelocks were picked up from the battlefield, but only 190 broadswords were found. Even if some allowance is made for units which are known not to have carried broadswords, such as the 'French' regulars, this suggests that no more than one in five of the 1,000-odd Highlanders killed at Culloden were armed with broadswords.

This Jacobite Clansman is therefore armed only with a Spanish 1728 pattern firelock (.69 calibre), one of a cargo run ashore at Peterhead in north-east Scotland at the end of January 1746. Most of this consignment was subsequently captured in a daring raid on Corgarff Castle on 29 February, but a fair number of firelocks and bayonets (not to be confused with the older *Escopetas* landed in 1719) had evidently been issued, since three days after Culloden Cumberland ordered "French or Spanish firelocks or bayonets and cartridge boxes to be delivered . . . to Ensign Stewart of Lascelles' Regt.; he is to distribute them to the Prisoners of our Army released here".

1 "Culloden" tartan, as worn by a member of the Prince's staff at the battle; **2** purse or sporran; **3** musket balls; **4** flints; **5** wadding; **6** white cockade worn by Lord George Murray; **7** Jacobite badge; **8** The targe has been dated to c1700. The style and quality of the decoration is unusual but also of rather poor quality, suggesting that it may in fact have been one of those mass produced in Edinburgh during the Jacobite Army's brief occupation of the capital in 1745; **9** The cartridge box depicted here is a French *gargousier*, or belly-box. Traditionally, however, ammunition, or at least the balls, patches and any spare flints, were carried in the sporran. **10** dirk and sheath c,1744: **11** a set of sketches showing how the highlander dressed himself in his belted plaid.

Artist's Note: *This figure was reconstructed on the following principles: the man is a Gordon, and I have given him a belted plaid in Huntly tartan, which closely resembles MacRae, Ross, and one interestingly styled 'The Prince's Own', which has a genuine provenance going back to 1715. "Tradition shows it to have been in use during a considerable portion of the (18th) century by such families as Gordon, Brodie and Forbes, or at least the members of those touched with Jacobitism, who appear to have assumed this tartan in common . . . " (Notes by D.W. Stewart). The slight variations between the four tartans mentioned have been convincingly shown to have resulted from certain errors in recording throughout the 19th century. The tartan of the stockings is derived from so-called dress MacRae, which – again according to D.W. Stewart – is a direct reconstruction of a hose tartan of 1715 used by the MacRaes, and thus quite possibly by the Gordons as well.*

G: AT REST – THE POTTEROW PORT, EDINBURGH, 1745

Not surprisingly, the Highland Army's occupation of Edinburgh in 1745 came as a considerable shock to the capital's inhabitants, one of whom, Patrick Crichton of Woodhouselee, left the following description:

"I entered the town by the Bristo port, which I saw to my

Highland soldier with Lochaber axe. Interestingly, only two out of nearly 40 Clansmen sketched by the Penicuik artist are armed with this weapon. Note that he also appears to be wearing breeches. [Author's collection]

indignation in the keeping of these caterpillers. A boy stood with a rusty drawn sword, and two fellows with things licke guns of the 16 centurie sat on each syde the entry to the poors howse, and these were catching the vermin from ther lurking places abowt ther plaids and throwing them away. I said to Mr Jerdin, minister of Liberton, 'Ar these the scownderalls [who] have surprised Edinburgh by treachery?' He answered, 'I had reither seen it in the hands of Frenchmen, but the divell and the deep sea are both bad.'

"When I came to the head of the stairs [which] leads to the Parliament Closs I cowld scarce pass for throng, and the Parliament Closs was crowed with them, for they were to make the parad at reading the manefesto and declaration from the Cross. I saw from a window near the Cross, north syde of the High Street, this commick fars or tragic commody. All these mountain officers with there troupes in rank and fyle marched from the Parliament Closs down to surrownd the Cross, and with there bagpipes and loosie crew they maid a large circle from the end of the Luickenbooths to half way below the Cross to the Cowrt of Gaird, and non but the officers and speciall favowrits and one lady in dress were admitted within the ranges, I observed there armes: they were guns of diferent syses, and some of innormowows lengh, some with butts turned up lick a heren, some tyed with puck threed to the stock, some withowt locks and some matchlocks, some had swords over ther showlder instead of guns, one or two had pitchforks, and some bits of sythes upon poles with a cleek, some old Lochaber axes. The pipes plaid pibrowghs when they were making ther circle. Thus

Simon Fraser, Lord Lovat (1667-1747) An inveterate intriguer and by all accounts thoroughly poisonous, surprisingly living a relatively long life he was eventually executed, having ordered his Clan out in 1745. [Private Scottish collection]

"A blew silk colours with the Lovat arms *Sine Sanguine Victor*", probably the second of three taken at Culloden by Monro's 37th Foot. The third is unidentified but may have been the staff from which the Appin Regiment's colours were torn – and saved. The motto is not Lovat's and the colour has been reconstructed to display the arms of Charles Fraser of Inverallochie, the Aberdeenshire laird who actually led the Frasers at Culloden. [Author's collection]

they stood rownd 5 or six men deep. Perhaps there was a strategem in this appearance, to make us think they were a rabbell unarmed in this publick parad show, for a greate many old men and boys were mixed, and they certanly conceiled there best men and arms thus; for they have 1400 of the most daring and best melitia in Europe."

There is, in fact, no evidence that the Jacobites were concealing their best men and arms, for in the early days they were indeed lamentably armed. After the dramatic victory at Prestonpans, matters improved considerably: captured British Army firelocks and bayonets were issued to Gordon of Glenbucket's and Lord Ogilvy's regiments, and a considerable quantity of arms were landed by French ships.

This plate, depicting newly equipped members of John Gordon of Glenbucket's Regiment hanging about by the Potterrow Port, is based on a number of contemporary sketches of the Highland troops in Edinburgh, by an unknown artist from Penicuik. While some men carry broadswords and the occasional Lochaber axe, the great majority are armed with firelocks and bayonets. Glenbucket himself, escorted here by one of the Hussars, was described by an eyewitness to the subsequent march through England as "an old man much crouched, who rode on a little grey highland beast". This is well captured in one of the Penicuik sketches, which also shows him riding in a belted plaid, rather than the much more practical trews. His banner was one of the few to survive the rising and its aftermath.

H: COLD STEEL

Notwithstanding the widespread use of firearms during the '45, Highlanders are traditionally associated with edged weapons and, in particular, the basket-hilted broadsword, commonly (and accurately) referred to as the *claidheamh mor* or claymore. In practice, the use of swords was probably quite limited, confined largely to the 'gentlemen' who formed the front rank of a Clan regiment. Although literary sources dwell on the more romantic weapons such as blued steel blades, often bearing the entirely spurious signature of *Andrea Ferrara* (most blades appear to have been German in origin), more prosaic records and some contemporary illustrations reveal that the ordinary Clansmen standing behind them normally had bows, spears or axes, and later firelocks and bayonets.

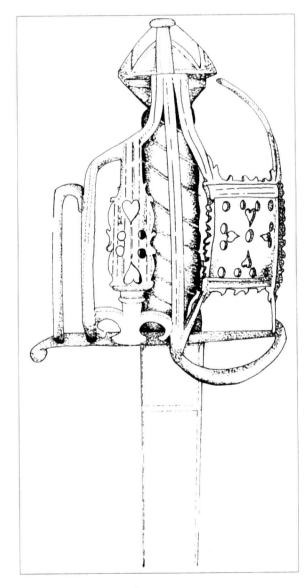

Typical example of the classic '*Glasgow*' style of broadsword hilt. [Author's collection]

The two-handed sword, or *claidheamh da laimh*, appears to have been most common in the 16th and 17th centuries. It was initially a scaled-up version of ordinary broadsword type, with angled quillons – as appears on a number of mediaeval Highland gravestones. Elsewhere in Europe the two-handed sword was essentially a specialist weapon, and this was probably the case in Scotland too. Eyewitnesses were understandably impressed with these swords, but their use does not appear to have been particularly widespread; most appear to have ended up as ceremonial bearing swords (which might again point to specialist use, by bodyguards). Illustrated here is the 'classic' 16th century form, with its distinctive sharply angled quillons, and a later, less attractive looking version with clam-shell guards.

Highland axes are almost invariably referred to as 'Lochaber' axes, but there were several types. The true Lochaber axe, of which a number of examples are depicted here, was essentially a form of halberd comprising a spiked head fixed on a pole. According to contemporary illustrations from both sides of the Irish sea, they varied in length between four and six feet and probably corresponded to the height of their owner. On one side of the head was a curved blade – initially quite small – and on the other a curved spike, traditionally used to dismount cavalrymen or cut their reins. Appropriately enough, the Scots word for this feature was *cleek*, which can mean 'hook' but is more accurately translated as 'claw'. In time the blade increased in size, the *cleek* became more pronounced and the spike disappeared entirely. The "bits of sythe upon a pole with a cleek" noted by Woodhouselee may actually have been variant styles of Lochaber axe rather than hasty improvisations. Ironically, the ultimate form of this particular weapon, and the one most readily associated with the name, actually appears to have originated in Aberdeen, once a noted source of such weapons. On 17 October 1715 an order arrived there from the Earl of Mar, "ordering and requyring the magistrats of Aberdeen to cause make three hundred Lochaber axes, and to send them to the camp at Perth, or where the army should be at the tyme . . . "

The basket-hilted broadsword or *claidheamh more* first appeared in a recognisable form in about the mid 16th century and was fully developed by the first quarter of the 18th century. It did not, as is often assumed, replace the two-handed *claidheamh da laimh*, but was simply a development of the much commoner quilloned broadsword. The low survival rate for these earlier weapons simply reflects the fact that blades were expensive and so were recycled, either by refitting them with basket hilts or by cutting them down into dirks (the latter apparently was common practice). Normally the blade was double-edged, but single-edged backswords do exist. The vast majority are straight bladed, but there are two variations. The *Turcael* had a curved or 'Turkish' blade (as carried by Alasdair Mor Grant in Plate A and by Charles Stewart of Ardsheal in 1745). Oddly enough this style briefly resurfaced in the early 19th century, carried by the flank company officers of Highland regiments (just as their counterparts in ordinary regiments carried sabres in place of the regulation straight-bladed thrusting sword carried by battalion or centre company officers). The other type featured a straight blade with serrated edges, like some 16th century Landsknecht swords. A sword of this style, called *The Brindled Wrangler*, was carried by Allan Cameron of Erracht, who went onto raise the 79th (Cameron) Highlanders in 1794.

Items shown here are as follows: **1** Irish-style *tuagh* or battle-axe from Inverlochy c.1645; **2** 17th century battle-axe; **3** Lochaber axes; **4** 15th century "Danish" axe; **5** socketed spear/ pikeheads of the 15th-17th century; **6** *claidheamh da laimh* of the 16th century; **7** *claidheamh da laimh* 17th century; **8** basket hilts of the 16th and early 19th century, with **8b** sketched variations on the design. **9a** details the basket hilt itself, and (**b**) exploded view of sword construction.

I: BATTLE (1) AULDEARN 1645

In Gaelic literature battles are invariably heroic affairs, none more so perhaps than the epic struggle of Alasdair MacCholla at Auldearn, early on the morning of 9 May 1645. MacCholla, as his name suggests, was a younger son of Coll MacGillespie MacDonald, better known as Coll Ciotach – by which nickname, anglicised as 'Colkitto' both father and son are confused. Coll Ciotach had held lands on Colonsay, latterly from Lord Lorne (later the Marquis of Argyle), but in 1639 he was arrested after becoming involved in the Earl of Antrim's plans for an invasion of Scotland on behalf of King Charles I. Alasdair MacCholla remained at large, however, and ended up in Ireland, where he managed to change sides twice in the bitter rebellion which broke out in 1641.

In 1644 Antrim's plan for a landing in Scotland was revived, this time in concert with an uprising to be led by the Marquis

Another survival of Culloden, this white banner bearing the Gordon arms was carried by John Gordon of Glenbucket's Regiment at Culloden. As it bears a gold coronet above the arms, it may originally have been carried by the Duke of Gordon's Regiment in 1715, since Glenbucket was his lieutenant-colonel. [Author's collection]

Sir Stuart Thriepland of Fingask (1716-1805). Despite his array of weapons, this Perthshire laird served in a medical capacity during the '45 and after a period of exile in France eventually became president of the Royal College of Physicians in Edinburgh. [Private Scottish collection]

of Montrose. At the end of June three regiments were shipped from Waterford under the command of Alasdair MacCholla. Most of the officers and men serving in these regiments were Irishmen and Anglo-Irish Royalists, armed with short pikes – a traditional Irish weapon – and muskets. Included among them, however, were a couple of companies of Hebrideans, who formed MacCholla's 'Lifeguard'.

At the beginning of May 1645 Montrose attempted to pin down a rather weak force led by Sir John Hurry. However, Hurry, an experienced soldier, retired westwards towards his base at Inverness. By the night of 8 May it had become clear that the Royalists were not going to catch him, and Montrose ordered his men to halt and bivouac in and around the village of Auldearn. That night Hurry linked up with the Inverness garrison and some other northern levies and abruptly swung back on his tracks to mount a full-scale assault on the sleeping Royalists at first light.

Roused just in time, Alasdair MacCholla and his Lifeguard, supported by William Gordon of Monymore's newly raised regiment – the only troops immediately at hand – adopted a blocking position on a low hill immediately to the west of the village. They tried to delay Hurry's advance while the rest of the army assembled. A brief firefight took place and MacCholla's ensign was slain. Although his yellow banner was quickly raised again, three more men were shot down in quick succession while carrying it. Hopelessly outnumbered and hindered rather than helped by the unsteady Gordon recruits, MacCholla fell back into the village and defended it

manfully against Sir Mungo Campbell of Lawers' Regiment. Although raised in the Highlands, the latter was a regular unit equipped with pikes and muskets, but posted behind them and shooting over their heads were some bowmen from Lewis, under the Earl of Seaforth's command.

Unable to maintain effective control of his men among the houses and yards, MacCholla twice attempted to counter-attack and was twice driven back. Hemmed in by pikemen, who thrust their weapons into his targe, he hacked off the pikeheads, but in the process broke his sword (according to one account he broke two in succession). At any rate, he was promptly handed another by his brother-in-law, who was himself cut down, and regained the doubtful security of one of the houses.

Meanwhile, another of his men, Ranald MacDomniull (or MacKinnon), pistolled one of the advancing pikemen, but then a Lewisman shot an arrow through both his cheeks. Dropping the empty pistol Ranald then tried to draw his sword, only to find it had stuck in the scabbard. Unable to protect himself, he received a number of superficial pike

Leanach Cottage, Culloden Moor. Although it stands on the site of the original Leanach steading and is often said to have been standing there during the battle, this cottage was actually built in about 1760 and provides a good example of the type of house occupied by a tenant farmer. [Author's collection]

Highlanders arresting a woman in an Edinburgh street. Note that both are armed with firelocks and bayonets.
[Author's collection]

BALVRAID

FROM INVERNESS

wounds before he could eventually get it out and run back to the nearest house where he could hear MacCholla roundly cursing the reluctant Gordons. By now MacCholla and his Lifeguard had given themselves up for lost but were determined to go down fighting to the last.

Fortunately the fight for the Auldearn was absorbing all Hurry's attention. Indeed. not only had his attack stalled, but his army had not even properly deployed. Instead, the regiments were simply standing stacked up behind the combatants struggling for possession of the village. Montrose hurriedly pulled the rest of the Royalist army together and mounted a series of counter-attacks. First his cavalry attacked on both flanks. This was then followed up by the veteran Strathbogie Regiment swinging around the southern end of the village and crashing into Lawers' men. This was the beginning of the end, and although it was the counter-attacks by the Gordon regiments that won the battle, none of it would have been possible without MacCholla's stand in the village and afterwards his epic fight was saluted by the Gaelic bards – unfortunately the authorship is unknow: *Alasdair . . . you were good that day at Auldearn, when you leapt among the pikes; and whether good or ill befell you, you would not shout 'Relief'*

Another description is attributed to Ian Lom: *Health and joy to the valiant Alasdair who won the battle of Auldearn with his army; You were not a feeble poltroon engaging in the crossing of swords when you were in the enclosure alone. Helmeted men with pikes in their hands were attacking you with all their might until you were relieved by Montrose.*

J: BATTLE (2) CULLODEN 1746

If MacCholla's stand at Auldearn may be taken as representative of the 'Heroic' view of Gaelic warfare, the experience of

Charles Stewart of Ardsheal's Appin Regiment a century later represents the grim reality as experienced by the ordinary Clansmen.

The regiment joined the Jacobite Army in Invergarry in August 1745 and its first engagement was Prestonpans on 21 September 1745. The precise number of casualties suffered in that famous victory is impossible to ascertain, but one officer, Captain Robert Stewart, was killed and three men, Donald MacDonald, Dougal Stewart and John Stewart, were left behind in the Edinburgh Royal Infirmary when the rebels marched south to Derby. Casualties may have been heavier in the drawn battle at Falkirk in January for at least one officer, also named Captain Robert Stewart, was killed there, two others wounded and two taken prisoner. Nevertheless, although both sets of figures almost certainly

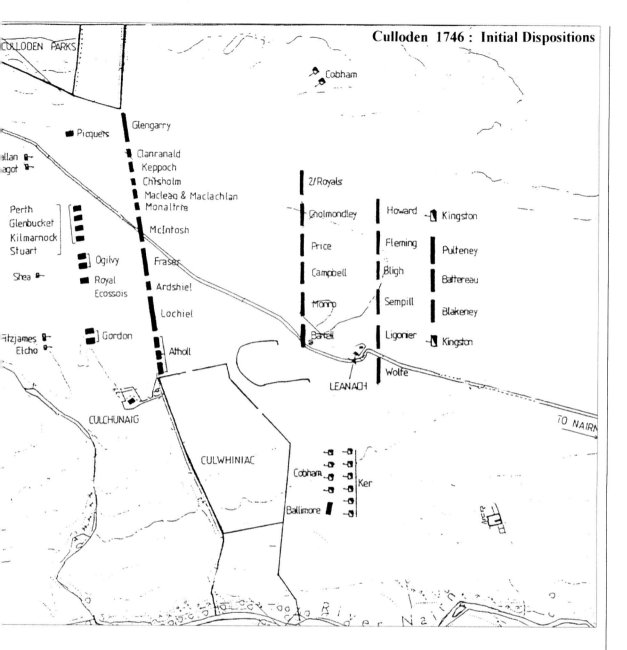

CULLODEN PARKS

Cobham

Picquets

Glengarry

allan

agot

Clanranald

Keppoch

Ch'sholm

Macleao & Maclachlan

Monaltrie

2/Royals

Perth
Glenbucket
Kilmarnock
Stuart

McIntosh

Cholmondley

Howard

Kingston

Shea

Ogilvy

Fraser

Price

Fleming

Pulteney

Royal
Ecossois

Ardshiel

Campbell

Bligh

Battereau

Lochiel

Monro

Sempill

Blakeney

Fitzjames
Etcho

Gordon

Barrell

Ligonier

Kingston

Atholl

LEANACH

Wolfe

CULCHUNAIG

TO NAIRN

CULWHINIAC

Cobham

Ker

Ballimore

River Nairn

Culloden Moor, 16 April 1746 (all unit frontages are to scale). The location and extent of the Culwhiniac and Leanach enclosures were originally plotted from contemporary maps and clues on the ground, but they have now been confirmed by geophysical survey. Note that the battlefield is considerably larger than depicted in most modern maps. [Author's collection]

give an incomplete picture of the actual losses, there is no doubt that whatever the true figures, they pale into insignificance in comparison to the regiment's casualty list from Culloden.

At the outset of the action Ardsheal and his men, shown here as depicted in a lively sketch by the Penicuick artist, stood on the right of the Jacobite front line, with Lochiel's Camerons on their immediate right and latterly John Roy Stuart's Regiment on their left. Thomas Sandby, who served on Cumberland's staff afterwards, produced a plan of the battle and appended to it a list of Jacobite regiments which appears to have been based on captured returns. This credits the Appin Regiment with a strength of no more than 150 men, excluding officers, on the day of the battle.

In the course of the last Highland Charge, Ardsheal's men

initially went straight forward, but then, like all too many of the other regiments on that wing, they followed the Camerons in a vain attempt to exploit the breakthrough momentarily created by the collapse of Barrell's 4th Foot. As a result, they were very badly shot up by Monro's 37th Foot (**see Warrior 18: British Redcoat 1**) and narrowly avoided losing their colours – a yellow saltire on a blue field.

Highland swordsman with Turkish blade.
[Author's collection]

For once it is possible to put an accurate figure on the regiment's losses at Culloden, thanks to the survival of a unique document. On 2 May 1746 two French frigates, the *Mars* and the *Bellona*, landed £35,000 in gold at Loch nan Uamh. At a meeting of most of the surviving Jacobite leaders at Muirlaggan on 8 May, it was decided to bring their regiments to a rendezvous at Invermallie ten days later, with a view to resuming the campaign. In the meantime it was agreed that part of the French gold should be distributed as back pay and as compensation to the wounded and to the relatives of those killed at Culloden. In the event, although the rendezvous did take place, albeit a week later than planned, the attempt to revive the rising failed. There is no evidence that Ardsheal brought any of his men to Invermallie, or for that matter even took part in the earlier conference at Muirlaggan, and perhaps for that reason the casualty list compiled by Stewart of Invernahyle was never presented. It makes grim reading, but at the same time provides an interesting insight into how a Clan regiment was brought together.

In total nine members of Ardsheal's family (a very broad category which included distant cousins) were killed and three others wounded. Two members of Stewart of Fasnacloich's family were killed and four wounded, including his uncle and two sons. Achnacone lost two brothers killed, while Captain Alexander Stewart of Invernahyle lost a nephew and three others and was himself wounded, along with his brother and 10 other members of his family. Five named individuals, all described as 'followers of Appin', were

returned as killed and six were wounded. All of these, 22 killed and 25 wounded in total, represented the Highland gentlemen, those who could be expected to have stood in the front rank armed with broadsword and targe. Almost all of them also appear, not entirely coincidentally, to have been officers.

A further 68 "Commoners" were killed and 40 wounded at Culloden, though sadly they are unidentified save by their surnames – 18 McColls, 13 Maclarens, 6 Carmichaels, 5 McIntyres, 4 McInnises and so on. Interestingly none of them actually bears the surname Stewart (although other common men taken prisoner during or after the rising do), which rather supports the idea that a Clan was in reality comprised of a warrior aristocracy "all of a name" and a very mixed bag of more or less hapless tenantry. It is also interesting to note that the gentlemen accounted for one quarter of those killed and a third of the wounded, which agrees pretty well with the proportion postulated by General Hawley

Chillingly the grand total comes to 155 officers and men dead or wounded, which may or may not include a further eight men taken prisoner. Sandby's "morning state" figure it will be remembered allowed only 150 rank and file. At least 20 officers and volunteers can be added to this figure, but even so it is clear that just over half of all the men serving in the regiment at Culloden were killed, and that very few of the remainder can have escaped unhurt.

K: HIGHLAND MERCENARIES 1746 – 1753

The dramatic explosion of blue bonneted Highland regiments in the wake of the last Jacobite Rising obscures the fact that from time immemorial substantial numbers of Highlanders had chosen, as individuals, to turn their backs on their Clan chiefs and go soldiering far beyond the hills. Up until the end of the 16th century most of them sought mercenary service in Ireland, first as Gallowglasses, taking service directly under the Irish Lords, but latterly in roving bands collectively referred to as "Redshanks" – a half contemptuous nickname alluding to their bare legs. After the Union of the Crowns, in 1603, and the simultaneous but unconnected ending of the Tudor conquest of Ireland, such mercenaries were forced to go further afield in search of employment. Recruiting parties organised by military contractors such as Donald, Lord Reay (otherwise the Chief of Mackay) or sent home by Scottish regiments in foreign armies became a common sight in the Highlands during the 17th century. With few exceptions, the men they enlisted were all of them readily assimilated into regular units such as the Dutch Army's famous Scotch Brigade, dressed, armed and trained for conventional warfare. Even as early as December 1552 two Highland companies levied for service on France under the Earl of Huntly were ordered to be "substantiouslie accompturit with jack and plait, steilbonnet, sword, bucklair,... and ane speir of sax elne [6 m] long or thairby".

During the 18th century many more Highlanders inevitably joined the British Army, and throughout the century a considerable number of officers and men serving in the 1st or Royal Regiment (now the Royal Scots) were noted to be Highlanders. This particular individual belongs to the rival French *Royal Ecossois*, however.

An ordinance was issued for the raising of the regiment on 3 December 1743 and the first officers' commissions were signed on 1 August 1744. Initially it was built up around a cadre drawn from the French Army's Irish Brigade and from British deserters, but Lord John Drummond was reported to be recruiting for his new regiment in the Highlands that summer. At the end of November 1745 he landed it in Scotland to aid the Jacobite insurgents, and a second battalion was authorised to be raised there in February 1746. At Culloden the regiment fought well and helped cover the retreat of the Jacobite right. An attempt by the Argyll Militia to intercept their withdrawal was brushed off easily, but in the process one battalion of the regiment was surrounded by dragoons and forced to surrender, although the other, with the colours, got away to Ruthven Barracks and did not surrender until 19 April. Afterwards, although most of the 1st Battalion personnel appear to have been treated as prisoners of war, having been enlisted *before* the regiment came to Scotland, some of the 2nd Battalion officers were tried as rebels. With the exception of one man, found to be a British Army deserter, all were eventually released.

This very distinctive Scottish uniform was described by a witness at the trial of one of the 2nd Battalion officers, Lieutenant Charles Oliphant: "Prisoner wore the uniform of Lord John Drummond's officers, viz; short blue coats, red vests laced with bonnets and white cockades." Unfortunately, none of the descriptions mentions the breeches worn. They may have been the white ones depicted here and described in 1757, although the 1753 Register does mention red ones as shown in the detail. An uncorroborated secondary source also refers to the grenadier company wearing plaids instead of breeches, and although this cannot be substantiated, at least one officer, James Cameron of Locheil, chose to wear a plaid with his regimentals when having his portrait painted in 1762.

The two battalions appear to have been consolidated in August 1747, and a more conventional uniform was adopted, items of which are shown here. There was a longer coat and a cocked hat in place of the blue bonnet, but they retained their cuffs *à l'ecossois* until their disbandment at the end of 1762.

Two other notionally Scottish regiments were raised in France after the collapse of the '45. The *Regiment d'Ogilvy* was authorised in February 1747, put together largely from Jacobite fugitives, including a fair number of officers who had served under Ogilvy in the two battalions which he led in Scotland. This regiment was clothed in a very similar fashion to the *Royal Ecossois* but was distinguished by having yellow rather than white lace and latterly by the wearing of red breeches. Like the *Royal Ecossois*, it was disbanded in 1762 and its personnel drafted into the Irish Brigade. The third of the Scottish units, the *Regiment d'Albany*, was authorised in October 1747, mainly, it seems, to provide a living for Cameron of Locheil, for it had few Scots in the ranks besides the officers and was disbanded in the following year. According to Lord Elcho its uniform was red with white facings.

The two main figures are from the *Royal Ecossois;* **1** serving in 1746, whilst **2** shows slight variations in dress by 1753. **3** *Royal Ecossois* regimental colour; **4** French army knapsack; **5** "neccessaries" bag and typical contents; **6** *giberne* or cartridge box; **7** internal wood and leather block for cartridge box; **8** cartridge and flints; **9** French military shirt; **10** French military breeches, with knee buckle; and **11** the basic footwear of the time with buckle.

L: AFTERWARDS – DUCHESS JEAN RECRUITING FOR THE GORDONS 1794

While a number of measures to curb the assumed warlike propensities of the Highland Clans were introduced in the wake of the '45, they were probably unnecessary, for most of the chiefs had remained loyal to King George and those who had sided with the Pretender were either dead, imprisoned or in exile. The Clans would certainly not have risen again.

There were still plenty of footloose young men willing to go soldiering rather than labour on farms. Recruits were for a time still sought, more or less clandestinely for the French service – though just how clandestine this activity really was is open to doubt, since the celebrated Allan Breck Stewart was openly wearing the uniform of the *Regiment d'Ogilvy* at the time of the Appin murder in 1752. Official licences were also still issued to officers enlisting men for the Dutch service throughout most of the 18th century. Nevertheless, the British Army was the biggest beneficiary. For the first ten years or so after the rising, recruitment of Highlanders was, as before, a fairly casual affair: small parties made the rounds of the markets, picking up a volunteer here or there for a particular corps.

In 1757 this situation changed abruptly with the outbreak of the Seven Years War and the consequent rapid expansion of the army. New regiments were required and were for the most part raised for rank, including Simon Fraser's 2nd

General Simon Fraser (1736-82). Just as slippery as his father, Lord Lovat, he commanded a Jacobite regiment in the '45 but managed to change sides at Culloden and eventually became a general in the British Army. [Private collection]

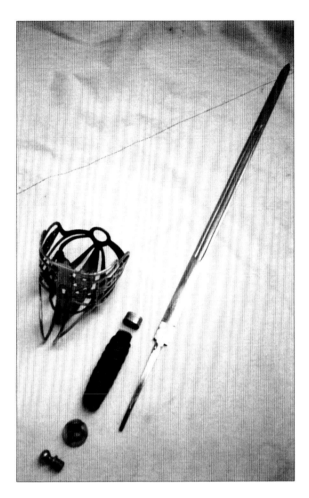

ABOVE **Components of an 1828 pattern basket-hilted broadsword. [Author's collection]**

Highland Battalion. Fraser, sometime Master of Lovat and a colonel in the Jacobite Army, appears to have succeeded in changing sides during the battle of Culloden and afterwards became a protégé of the Duke of Argyll. In 1752 he had served as a prosecutor in the infamous Appin murder trial. By way of reward, he was given the opportunity to complete his official rehabilitation by raising a regiment. This he did in a remarkably short time, providing the officers from other former Jacobites or at least their sons. They seem to have very largely found their men in the old way, by taking their tenants' sons, as their fathers had done for generations. Suitably encouraged by this dramatic success and the unquestioned assumption that all Highlanders were naturally warlike, the Government went on to authorise the raising of other kilted regiments.

At first the response was good, but towards the end of the 18th century it became increasingly difficult for the chiefs to raise their men as before. In the first place there was simply a limit to the number of young men who were willing to go soldiering. A Clan regiment before Culloden was in a sense a militia: the men of the Clan could be called out either to defend their lands or to go raiding somebody else's. Calling them out to become professional soldiers was a different matter entirely.

The natural response to such reluctance was to offer inducements such as greater security of tenure, and ultimately to offer cash bounties; eventually this destroyed the bonds of the Clan system. Where once a Clansman might have followed his own chief, however reluctantly, precisely because he was his chief, now he was encouraged to follow another for gold. With the country awash with predatory recruiters, each offering a bigger bounty than the last, it was foolish not to look around and accept the best offer.

When the young Marquis of Huntly was granted Letters of Service to raise the 100th (Gordon) Highlanders on 10 February 1794, his mother, Duchess Jean, enthusiastically set about helping him to raise it, famously offering a kiss and a guinea to every recruit. It makes a fine tale, and by all accounts created something of a stir at the time, but something of the reality behind it may be seen in a report by one of the regiment's recruiting agents at Aberdeen, Captain Finlason:

"March 11 – This day I engaged George Gordon from the Cabrach, late a tenant of the Duke. He was dislodged by Coinachie or Mr. Bell, and says he has £48 due him on bills from good men for the stocking of his farm sold. He is a tight Light Infantry man, 26 [years of] age. But I had him engage thro' many windings – 1. a recommendation to the Marquis to sollicit the Duke for his former tack [lease] to him on or after his discharge from the army: 2. an application to you or Mr. Bell for some tenement or bigging for his wife till his return: 3. promotion if he deserves it: besides 4. ten guineas bounty and three guineas to his pilot, Sergeant Reid. This hero of the Cabrach says he is highly related here, viz to the Rev. Mr. Sheriffs and his brother the advocate. Tomorrow he goes in high dress with his sword by his side to announce his new profession."

One can only marvel that he did not insist on his kiss from the Duchess as well, but at any rate, with or without his father's old sword, he may not have been much of a bargain, for the original muster rolls show that George Gordon from the Cabrach was indeed attested on 12 March 1794 and at 5ft 4in tall he may well have been a "tight Light Infantry man", but he is also described in the roll as a labourer, and appears to have been discharged shortly afterwards. Whether he regained his lease from the Duke is not known.

LEFT **The end of it all – one of the grave markers for the defeated Jacobites on Culloden Moor. [Author's collection]**

PLACES OF INTEREST

Visiting Culloden Moor is essential for anyone interested in the Highland Clans. Situated outside Inverness, it is easily accessible by road and, on a fine day, by a bracing walk from Inverness itself (downhill on the way back). The National Trust for Scotland, which owns approximately a quarter of the battlefield, has removed an intrusive forestry plantation and reconstructed the turf and stone enclosure walls on the south-east side of the moor. However, the battlefield as laid out is far too small and the regimental markers are wrongly placed. Beware claims that the Leanach cottage was standing in 1746 and that Jacobite wounded were burned alive in an adjacent barn. The steading was actually a British Army field hospital!

A short distance away from Culloden is Fort George at Ardersier. Still in full-time use by the army, this 18th century fort and barrack complex, built after the '45, is also open to the public.

Down the A9 from Inverness is the Highland Folk Museum at Kingussie and the adjacent Ruthven Barracks, scene of two short sieges during the '45.

Also on the A9 is the battlefield of Killiecrankie. The National Trust visitor centre in the pass does not lie on the battlefield, which is itself crossed by the A9. Travelling northwards the road actually runs along the narrow Urrard plateau on which General Mackay formed his army. The Jacobite Army was formed on a narrower ridge-line or shelf higher up the hill to the right of the road. The only part of Mackay's position undisturbed by roadworks is a small birch wood occupied by Colonel Lauder's grenadier detachment, on Mackay's extreme left.

Outside Edinburgh the battlefield of Prestonpans has largely been covered by industrial and residential development, but Colonel Gardiner's house has recently been restored magnificently.

BIBLIOGRAPHY

Anderson, Peter, *Culloden Moor and the Story of the Battle*
(Stirling 1920)

Baynes, John, *The Jacobite Rising of 1715* (London 1970)

Brown, I.A., & Cheape, H., *Witness to Rebellion: John Maclean's Journal of the Forty-five and the Penicuik Drawings* (East Linton 1996)

Bumsted, J., *The People's Clearance: Highland Emigration to British North America 1770-1815* (Edinburgh 1982)

Burt, E., *Letters from a Gentleman in the North of Scotland* (London 1754)

Caldwell, David (Ed.), *Scottish Weapons and Fortifications 1100-1800*
(Edinburgh 1981)

Dunbar, J.T., *History of Highland Dress* (London 1979); *The Costume of Scotland* (London 1984)

Grimble, Ian, *Chief of Mackay* (Edinburgh 1993)

Home, John, *History of the Rebellion in the `Year 1745* (London 1802)

Hopkins, Paul, *Glencoe and the End of the Highland War*
(Edinburgh 1986)

Livingston, A (and others), *Muster Roll of Prince Charles Edward Stuart's Army* (Aberdeen 1984)

McClintock, H.F., *Old Irish and Highland Dress* (Dundalk 1950)

Mackay, W., *Urquhart and Glenmoriston* (Inverness 1914)

Prebble, John, *Mutiny: Highland Regiments in Revolt 1743-1804* (London 1975); *Culloden* (London 1961); *Glencoe* (London 1966)

Reid, Stuart, *Like Hungry Wolves: Culloden Moor 16th April 1746* (London 1994); *1745: A Military History* (Tunbridge Wells 1996); *18th Century Highlanders* (London 1993); *The Campaigns of Montrose* (Edinburgh 1990)

Spalding, John, *Memorialls of the Trubles in Scotland 1627-1645*
(Aberdeen 1850-51)

Stevenson, David, *Highland Warrior: Alasdair MacCholla and the Civil Wars* (Edinburgh 1994)

Stewart, David, of Garth, *Sketches of the Highlanders of Scotland*
(Edinburgh 1822)

Tayler, A & H., *Jacobites of Aberdeenshire & Banffshire in the '45* (Aberdeen 1928)

Interpreters

Wallace Clan Trust, Clan Studios, Kingston, Glasgow, Strathclyde G5 8TA

The Watch: 43rd – 42nd Highland Regiment, 52 Balcombe Road,
Horley, Surrey RH6 9AA

Royal Ecossois: 1 Golden Noble Hill, Colchester, Essex

INDEX

References to illustrations are shown in **bold**. Plates are prefixed 'pl.' with caption locators in brackets, e.g. 'pl. **J2**(62).